# THE HERITAGE OF AMERICA

# THE HERITAGE OF
# AMERICA

*Edited by*

HENRY STEELE COMMAGER

*and*

ALLAN NEVINS

REVISED AND ENLARGED EDITION

ILLUSTRATED

Little, Brown and Company · Boston
1951

*Published September 1939*
*Reprinted September 1939*
*Reprinted October 1939*
*Reprinted November 1939*
*Reprinted June 1945*
*Reprinted January 1947*
*Revised October 1949*
*Reprinted March 1950*

PRINTED IN THE UNITED STATES OF AMERICA BY
KINGSPORT PRESS, INC., KINGSPORT, TENNESSEE

*To*

N. T. McC. C.

A. N.

M. N.

H. S. C., Jr.

# Introduction

FEW men realize how much history has been made in America since the first explorers and colonists reached its shores; how broad, how richly multiform, how full of adventure, drama, and color this history has been. Few realize, again, how much of this history has been written by actual participants and observers; how many thousands of racy, vivid, and veracious narratives have been penned by the settlers, the soldiers, the traders, the boatmen, the gold hunters, the fur trappers, the railroad builders, the merchants, the educators, the preachers, the politicians. The writers of such narratives range from Presidents to pioneers, from millionaires to mule drivers, from admirals to aviators. In general usage the connotation of the word history tends always to become too formal, and many men tend to think of it too much as a subject connected with the dusty library and the full-dress treatise. That is an error which cannot be too often corrected. History is not a matter of libraries but of life; the best of it is not stiffly secondhand, but is matter pulsing with the hopes and despairs, the ardors and endurances, the joys and sorrows of plain people everywhere. The editors of this volume hope that it will do something to demonstrate this fact. They hope that it will contribute to an understanding of the variety, the vitality, and the absorbing interest of that immense part of our historical literature which has come from the pens of the men and women who helped to make history.

From the great treasure house of firsthand narratives of American life many volumes like this might be selected. Our book is meant to be but a sampling of the feast that lies spread for all who will come to partake of it. We hope that many who are within reach of books will be led by these pages to explore further for themselves. For those others who do not find large libraries available, we hope this book will serve a special purpose, for it will supply typical extracts from a large body of writers, some of whom are not easily found. We make no claim that this is the best possible collection. No collection can be "best" for any but a limited group. We offer it merely as a catholic and fairly comprehensive garner, representative of what we ourselves have found most illuminating and delightful, and in our opinion adapted to seize the interest and awaken the imagination of a large body of readers. In choosing selections we have applied various touchstones. But the principal test, beyond our insistence upon a reasonable accuracy and authenticity, has always been that of broad human interest. The volume is not for the specialist, and does not fall into or even touch that category of "collected documents" or "source books" of which large numbers already exist. At the same time, we hope that it will afford instruction to students as well as pleasure to general readers.

No collection of personal narratives, no matter how extensive, can ever form a really connected history of America. Many personal narratives present a tangential interest. Dealing with a more or less unique experience, they lie somewhat apart from the general stream of affairs, or traverse it at an angle. But we have tried hard to give this book as much coherence and integration as possible. We have divided it into sections, each representing a different phase or era of American life; and within each section we have tried to place a group of narratives that have some relation to each other, and that taken together really give some conception of this phase or era. Enough editorial matter has been supplied to form a background, and to offer a measure of continuity. We believe that the book can be read from beginning to end without any sense of undue roughness, any consciousness of glaring gaps; and that is surely sufficient. Had we increased the amount of editorial matter, we would have found ourselves writing another general history of America, and there are assuredly enough general histories of an elementary nature already.

Our guiding rule in dealing with the text of these narratives has been to serve the general reader and the ordinary student, not to minister to the pedant. We have tried to insist upon verbal accuracy. We have made spelling and punctuation conform to modern usage, however, and we have omitted ellipsis marks in the interest of readability. At the end of the volume we offer a full bibliography, so that those who wish to obtain the text of any selection in its original form may do so. To the many publishers and authors who have cordially co-operated with us, and whose favors are specifically acknowledged elsewhere in this book, we desire here to express our warm gratitude. We of course wish it understood that none of the views expressed by the various writers included in the volume is necessarily our own; indeed, we have tried to obtain a wide variety of views, by no means excluding some of an extreme or eccentric character.

We gratefully acknowledge the services of Miss Margaret Carroll in helping to select and prepare for the press the contents of this volume.

HENRY STEELE COMMAGER<br>ALLAN NEVINS

*New York City,*

# Contents

## IV · White Men and Red

## V · The Struggle for the Continent

## VI · The Coming of the Revolution

## VII · The Winning of Independence

## VIII · *Confederation and Constitution*

## IX · *Launching the New Government*

## X · *The War of 1812*

## XI · *The Hardy Frontiersman*

## XII · New Settlements in the Wilderness

## XIII · Sailing and Whaling

## XIV · Steamboat Days

## XV · Social Life in the Early Republic

# XVI · Man the Reformer

# XVII · The South and Slavery

# XVIII · Abolition and Fugitive Slaves

# XIX · Westward the Course of Empire

## XX · The Mining Kingdom

## XXI · Texas and the Mexican War

## XXII · Politics

CONTENTS xvii

141. Carl Schurz Hears Lincoln Debate with Douglas 632
142. Abraham Lincoln Is Nominated in the Wigwam 637

## XXIII · O Captain, My Captain

143. "We Are Not Enemies, but Friends" 645
144. Mr. Lincoln Hammers Out a Cabinet 647
145. Nathaniel Hawthorne Sees President Lincoln 650
146. President Lincoln Pardons a Sleeping Sentinel 653
147. Lincoln Reads the Emancipation Proclamation 659
148. Secretary Chase Recalls a Famous Cabinet Meeting 661
149. Lincoln Frees the Slaves 664
150. Lincoln Consoles Mrs. Bixby 666
151. "With Malice toward None, with Charity for All" 666
152. President Lincoln Is Assassinated 668

## XXIV · Behind the Lines

153. Mr. Dicey Watches Recruiting on Boston Common 675
154. A War Clerk Describes the Confederate Cabinet 678
155. Writing "The Battle Hymn of the Republic" 681
156. A Hospital Transport Receives the Wounded 683
157. The Confederates Burn Their Cotton 687
158. The Yankees Sack Sarah Morgan Dawson's Home 689
159. Anna Dickinson Sees Draft Riots in New York City 696
160. President Davis Quells a Food Riot in Richmond 703
161. A War Clerk Suffers Scarcity in Richmond 705
162. Mr. Eggleston Recalls When Money Was Plentiful 711
163. Nevada Miners Bid on the "Sanitary" Flour Sack 715
164. Suffering in Andersonville Prison 719
165. The Disintegration of the Confederate Army 721

## XXV · The Blue and the Gray

166. Mrs. Chesnut Watches the Attack on Fort Sumter 729
167. Abner Doubleday Defends Fort Sumter 733

## XXVI · Reconstruction

## XXVII · The Last West

## XXXII · *The Progressive Era*

## XXXIII · *Modern Politics*

## XXXIV · *The World War*

## XXXV · From Normalcy to New Deal

## XXXVI · The Second World War

# Illustrations

# I

## Opening Up the Continent

Columbus Crossing the Ocean

# 1. Leif Ericson Sails to Vineland

*Columbus' voyages were not the first made to the American continents. In a geographical sense Greenland is part of America, and the Northmen began colonizing Greenland in the tenth century. Moreover, a true pre-Columbian discovery of the great mainland occurred in the year 1000 A.D. That summer Leif, the son of Eric the Red, set out from Greenland with thirty-five men to examine the lands to the south. "He was a large man and strong," says the saga, "of noble aspect, prudent and moderate in all things." He sailed south till he reached a bleak, stony land which was probably Labrador or northern Newfoundland; then on to a wooded coast which seems to have been Cape Breton Island or Nova Scotia, and which he called Markland; and then still farther south to a country — Vineland — so pleasant, warm, and full of fish that he resolved to spend the winter in it. His brother Thorvald made a voyage later in his track, while a wealthy Icelander directed an unsuccessful attempt to establish a colony in Vineland. The ships of the Northmen were probably stauncher and safer, and were certainly faster, than those of Columbus; but the Northmen lacked the geographical knowledge that would have enabled them to make real use of their discoveries, while Europe in the year 1000 had not reached a stage of progress which made the settling of America possible.*

THERE was now much talk about voyages of discovery. Leif, the son of Eric the Red, of Brattahild, went to Biarni Heriulfson, and bought the ship of him, and engaged men for it, so that there were thirty-five men in all. Leif asked his father Eric to be the leader on the voyage, but Eric excused himself, saying that he was now pretty well stricken in years, and could not now, as formerly, hold out all the hardships of the sea. Leif said that still he was the one of the family whom good fortune would soonest attend, and Eric gave in to Leif's request, and rode from home so soon as they were ready, and it was but a short way to the ship. The horse stumbled that Eric rode, and he fell off and bruised his foot. Then said Eric, "It is not ordained that I should discover more countries than that which we now inhabit, and we should make no further attempt in company." Eric went home to Brattahild, but Leif repaired to the ship, and his comrades with him, thirty-five men. There was a German on the voyage who was named Tyrker.

Now prepared they their ship, and sailed out into the sea when they were ready, and then found that land first which Biarni had found last. There sailed they to the land, and cast anchor, and put off boats and went ashore, and saw there no grass. Great icebergs were over all the up country, but like a plain of flat stones was all from the sea to the mountains, and it appeared to them that this land had no good qualities. . . .

Then went they on board, and after that sailed out to sea, and found another land. They sailed again to the land and cast anchor, then put off boats and went on shore. This land was flat and covered with wood, and white sands were far around where they went, and the shore was low. Then said Leif: "This land shall be named after its qualities, and called Markland [woodland]." They then immediately returned to the ship.

Now sailed they thence into the open sea with a northeast wind, and were two days at sea before they saw land, and they sailed thither and came to an island which lay to the eastward of the land, and went up there and looked round them in good weather, and observed that there was dew upon the grass. And it so happened that they touched the dew with their hands, and raised the fingers to the mouth, and they thought that they had never before tasted anything so sweet.

After that they went to the ship and sailed into a sound which lay between the island and a promontory which ran out to the eastward of the land, and then steered westward past the promontory. It was very shallow at ebb tide, and their ship stood up so that it was far to see from the ship to the water. But so much did they desire to land that they did not give themselves time to wait until the water again rose under their ship, but ran at once on shore at a place where a river flows out of a lake. But so soon as the waters rose up under the ship, then took they boats, and rowed to the ship, and floated it up the river, and thence into the lake, and there cast anchor, and brought up from the ship their skin cots, and made there booths.

After this they took counsel and formed the resolution of remaining there for the winter, and built there large houses. There was no want of salmon either in the river or in the lake, and larger salmon than they had before seen. The nature of the country was, as they thought, so good that cattle would not require house feeding in winter, for there came no frost in winter, and little did the grass wither there. Day and night were more equal than in Greenland or Iceland, for on the shortest day the sun was above the horizon from half past seven in the forenoon till half past four in the afternoon. . . .

It happened one evening that a man of the party was missing, and this was Tyrker the German. This Leif took much to heart, for Tyrker had been long with his father and him, and loved Leif much in his childhood. Leif now took his people severely to task, and prepared to seek for Tyrker, and took twelve men with him. But when they had got a short way from the house, then came Tyrker towards them and was joyfully received. Leif soon saw that his foster father was not in his right senses. . . . Then said Leif to him: "Why were thou so late, my fosterer, and separated from the party?" He now spoke first for a long time in German, and rolled his eyes about to different sides, and twisted his mouth, but they did not understand what he said. After a time he spoke Norsk. "I have not been much farther off, but still I have something new to tell of; I found vines and grapes." "But is that true, my fosterer?" quoth Leif. "Surely is it true," replied he, "for I was bred up in a land where there is no want of either vines or grapes."

They slept for the night, but in the morning Leif said to his sailors: "We will now set about two things, in that the one day we gather grapes, and the other day cut vines and fell trees, so from thence will be a loading for my ship." And that was the counsel taken, and it is said their longboat was filled with grapes. Now was a cargo cut down for the ship, and when the spring came they got ready and sailed away; and Leif gave the land a name after its qualities, and called it Vineland.

They sailed now into the open sea, and had a fair wind until they saw Greenland, and the mountains below the glaciers. . . .

Now there was much talk about Leif's voyage to Vineland; and Thorvald, his brother, thought that the land had been much too little explored. Then said Leif to Thorvald: "Thou canst go with my ship, brother, if thou wilt, to Vineland, but I wish first that the ship should go and fetch the timber which Thorer had upon the rock." And so it was done.

Now Thorvald made ready for this voyage with thirty men, and took counsel thereon with Leif, his brother. Then made they their ship ready, and put to sea . . . until they came to Leif's booths in Vineland. There they laid up their ship, and spent a pleasant winter, and caught fish for their support.

But in the spring, said Thorvald, they should make ready the ship, and some of the men should take the ship's longboat round the western part of the land, and explore there during the summer. To them the land appeared fair and woody, and but a short distance between the wood and the sea, and white sands; there were many islands and much shallow water. They found neither dwellings of men or beasts, except upon an island to the westward, where they found a corn shed of wood, but many works of men they found not. And they then went back and came to Leif's booths in the autumn.

Voyages of the Northmen to America

# 2. Christopher Columbus Discovers America

*No one knows what Columbus expected or wished to find when he set out on his immortal voyage. We do know that he was obsessed by the idea that the world was round, and that by sailing west he could reach the East. But did he expect to find old lands or new? Did he hope to find a shorter route to Oriental goods and spices, or vast populations to convert to Christianity, or new domains to be governed by Spain? At any rate, the Spanish sovereigns gave him a letter to the Grand Khan, and he returned from his first voyage reporting that he had reached Cipango or Japan and the Spice Islands. Columbus remains a shadowy per-*

*sonality; his birth, training, and ambitions all the subject of violent*
*controversy. But it is certain that he was dominated by the sense of*
*a high mission, and in character and intellect had many elements of*
*greatness. With ninety men, his three frail vessels left Palos before*
*sunrise on August 3, 1492. Refitting at the Canaries, they did not sail*
*again until September 6. As the voyage lengthened the temper of*
*the sailors grew more dangerous, and it was fortunate for Columbus*
*that early in October signs of land thickened.*

WEDNESDAY, 10th of October. — The course was west-southwest, and they went at the rate of ten miles an hour, occasionally
twelve miles, and sometimes seven. During the day and night
they made fifty-nine leagues, counted as no more than forty-four.
Here the people could endure no longer. They complained of the
length of the voyage. But the Admiral cheered them up in the
best way he could, giving them good hopes of the advantages they
might gain from it. He added that, however much they might complain, he had to go to the Indies, and that he would go on until
he found them, with the help of our Lord.

Thursday, 11th of October. — The course was west-southwest,
and there was more sea than there had been during the whole of
the voyage. They saw sandpipers, and a green reed near the ship.
Those of the caravel *Pinta* saw a cane and a pole, and they took up
another small pole which appeared to have been worked with iron;
also another bit of cane, a land plant, and a small board. The crew
of the caravel *Niña* also saw signs of land, and a small branch
covered with berries. Everyone breathed afresh and rejoiced at
these signs. The run until sunset was twenty-six leagues.

After sunset the Admiral returned to his original west course, and
they went along at the rate of twelve miles an hour. Up to two
hours after midnight they had gone ninety miles, equal to twenty-
two and a half leagues. As the caravel *Pinta* was a better sailer, and
went ahead of the Admiral, she found the land, and made the
signals ordered by the Admiral. The land was first seen by a sailor
named Rodrigo de Triana. But the Admiral, at ten in the previous
night, being on the castle of the poop, saw a light, though it was so
uncertain that he could not affirm it was land. He called Pedro

Gutierrez, a gentleman of the King's bedchamber, and said that there seemed to be a light, and that he should look at it. He did so, and saw it. The Admiral said the same to Rodrigo Sanchez of Segovia, whom the King and Queen had sent with the fleet as inspector, but he could see nothing, because he was not in a place whence anything could be seen. After the Admiral had spoken he saw the light once or twice, and it was like a wax candle rising and falling. It seemed to few to be an indication of land, but the Admiral made certain that land was close. When they said the *Salve,* which all the sailors were accustomed to sing in their way, the Admiral asked and admonished the men to keep a good lookout on the forecastle, and to watch well for land; and to him who should first cry out that he saw land, he would give a silk doublet, besides the other rewards promised by the sovereigns, which were ten thousand maravedis to him who should first see it. At two hours after midnight the land was sighted at a distance of two leagues. They shortened sail, and lay by under the mainsail without the bonnets.

Friday, 12th of October. — The vessels were hove to, waiting for daylight; and on Friday they arrived at a small island of the Lucayos, called, in the language of the Indians, Guanahani [Watling Island; named San Salvador by Columbus]. Presently they saw naked people. The Admiral went on shore in the armed boat, and Martin Alonso Pinzon, and Vicente Yañez, his brother, who was captain of the *Niña.* The Admiral took the royal standard, and the captains went with two banners of the green cross, which the Admiral took in all the ships as a sign, with an F and a Y [Fernando and Ysabel] and a crown over each letter, one on one side of the cross and the other on the other. Having landed, they saw trees very green, and much water, and fruits of diverse kinds. The Admiral called to the two captains, and to the others who leaped on shore, and said that they should bear faithful testimony that he, in presence of all, had taken, as he now took, possession of the said island for the King and for the Queen, his lords, making the declarations that are required, as is more largely set forth in the testimonies which were then made in writing.

Presently many inhabitants of the island assembled. What follows is in the actual words of the Admiral in his book of the first navigation and discovery of the Indies. "I," he says, "that we might form great friendship. for I knew that they were a people who could be more easily freed and converted to our holy faith by love than by force, gave to some of them red caps, and glass beads to put round their necks, and many other things of little value, which gave them great pleasure, and made them so much our friends that it was a marvel to see. They afterwards came to the ship's boats where we were, swimming and bringing us parrots, cotton threads in skeins, darts, and many other things; and we exchanged them for other things that we gave them, such as glass beads and small bells. In fine, they took all, and gave what they had with good will. It appeared to me to be a race of people very poor in everything. They go as naked as when their mothers bore them, and so do the women, although I did not see more than one young girl. All I saw were youths, none more than thirty years of age. They are very well made, with very handsome bodies, and very good countenances. Their hair is short and coarse, almost like the hairs of a horse's tail. They wear the hairs brought down to the eyebrows, except a few locks behind, which they wear long and never cut. They paint themselves black, and they are the color of the Canarians, neither black nor white. Some paint themselves white, others red, and others of what color they find. Some paint their faces, others the whole body, some only round the eyes, others only on the nose. They neither carry nor know anything of arms, for I showed them swords, and they took them by the blade and cut themselves through ignorance. They have no iron, their darts being wands without iron, some of them having a fish's tooth at the end, and others being pointed in various ways. They are all of fair stature and size, with good faces, and well made. I saw some with marks of wounds on their bodies, and I made signs to ask what it was, and they gave me to understand that people from other adjacent islands came with the intention of seizing them, and that they defended themselves. I believed, and still believe, that they come here from the mainland to take them prisoners. They should be good servants and intelligent, for I observed that they quickly took in what was said to them, and I believe that they would easily be made Christians, as it appeared to me that they had no religion. I, our Lord being pleased, will take hence, at the time of my departure, six natives for your Highnesses, that they may learn to speak. I saw no beast of any kind, except parrots, on this island." The above is in the words of the Admiral.

Journal of Christopher Columbus

# 3. De Soto Finds the Mississippi and Is Buried beneath It

*Hernando de Soto had served with Pizarro in the conquest of Peru and the looting of its incredible riches. Returning home, he was able in 1537 to obtain the royal appointment as Governor of Cuba, with authority to conquer all the unknown lands north of the Gulf of Mexico. Nobody but Pánfilo de Narváez had made a serious attempt to penetrate these lands, and De Narváez, setting forth in 1528, had lost his life and those of all but four of his four hundred followers. De Soto talked with one of these four survivors, Cabeza de Vaca, before he left Spain. He believed there must be kingdoms to conquer in the vast unknown expanse, and was especially excited by De Vaca's gossip about the Seven Cities. In the spring of 1539 he gathered at Havana nine vessels and 570 men. A little later he was fighting his way through the hostile tribesmen of the Creek Confederacy in what is now Alabama. In December, 1541, he reached the Yazoo, and there spent the winter. When spring came in 1542 he and his men crossed the Mississippi and wandered northward as far as present-day Missouri, looking in vain for El Dorado. Then they turned disconsolately southward again.*

THREE days having gone by since some maize had been sought after, and but little found in comparison with the great want there was of it, the Governor became obliged to move at once, notwithstanding the wounded had need of repose, to where there should be abundance. He accordingly set out for Quizquiz, and marched seven days through a wilderness having many pondy places, with thick forests, all fordable, however, on horseback, except some basins or lakes that were swum. He arrived at a town of Quizquiz without being descried, and seized all the people before they could come out of their houses. Among them was the mother of the cacique;

and the Governor sent word to him, by one of the captives, to come and receive her, with the rest he had taken. The answer he returned was that if his lordship would order them to be loosed and sent, he would come to visit and do him service.

The Governor, since his men arrived weary and likewise weak for want of maize, and the horses were also lean, determined to yield to the requirement and try to have peace; so the mother and the rest were ordered to be set free, and with words of kindness were dismissed. The next day, while he was hoping to see the chief, many Indians came with bows and arrows to set upon the Christians, when he commanded that all the armed horsemen should be mounted and in readiness. Finding them prepared, the Indians stopped at the distance of a crossbowshot from where the Governor was, near a river bank, where, after remaining quietly half an hour, six chiefs arrived at the camp, stating that they had come to find out what people it might be, for that they had knowledge from their ancestors that they were to be subdued by a white race; they consequently desired to return to the cacique to tell him that he should come presently to obey and serve the Governor. After presenting six or seven skins and shawls brought with them, they took their leave and returned with the others who were waiting for them by the shore. The cacique came not, nor sent another message.

There was little maize in the place, and the Governor moved to another town, half a league from the great river [the Mississippi], where it was found in sufficiency. He went to look at the river, and saw that near it there was much timber of which piraguas might be made, and a good situation in which the camp might be placed. He directly moved, built houses, and settled on a plain a crossbowshot from the water, bringing together there all the maize of the towns behind, that at once they might go to work and cut down trees for sawing out planks to build barges. . . .

The next day the cacique arrived, with two hundred canoes filled with men having weapons. They were painted with ocher, wearing great bunches of white and other plumes of many colors, having feathered shields in their hands, with which they sheltered the oarsmen on either side, the warriors standing erect from bow to stern, holding bows and arrows. The barge in which the cacique came had an awning at the poop under which he sat; and the like had the barges of the other chiefs; and there, from under the canopy where the chief man was, the course was directed and orders issued to the rest. All came down together and arrived within a stone's cast of the ravine, where the cacique said that he had come to visit, serve, and obey him, for he had heard that he was the greatest of lords, the most powerful on all the earth and that he must see what he would have him do. The Governor expressed his pleasure, and besought him to land that they might the better confer; but the chief gave no reply, ordering three barges to draw near, wherein was great quantity of fish, and loaves like bricks, made of the pulp of plums, which De Soto receiving, gave him thanks and again entreated him to land.

Making the gift had been a pretext to discover if any harm might be done, but finding the Governor and his people on their guard, the cacique began to draw off from the shore, when the crossbowmen who were in readiness, with loud cries, shot at the Indians, and struck down five or six of them. They retired with great order, not one leaving the oar, even though the one next to him might have fallen, and covering themselves, they withdrew. Afterwards they came many times and landed; when approached, they would go back to their barges. These were fine-looking men, very large and well formed; and what with the awnings, the plumes, and the shields, the pennons, and the number of people in the fleet, it appeared like a famous armada of galleys.

During the thirty days that were passed there, four piraguas were built, into three of which, one morning, three hours before daybreak, the Governor ordered twelve cavalry to enter — four in each — men in whom he had confidence that they would gain the land notwithstanding the Indians, and secure the passage, or die; he also sent some crossbowmen on foot with them, and in the other piragua oarsmen to take them to the opposite shore.

So soon as they had come to shore the piraguas returned; and when the sun was up two hours high, the people had all got over. The distance was near half a league; a man standing on the shore could not be told, whether he were a man or something else, from the other side. The stream was swift and very deep; the water, always flowing turbidly, brought along from above many trees and much timber, driven onward by its force. There were many fish of

several sorts, the greater part differing from those of the fresh
waters of Spain.

The Governor, conscious that the hour approached in which he
should depart this life, commanded that all the King's officers
should be called before him, the captains and the principal per-
sonages, to whom he made a speech. He said that he was about
to go into the presence of God, to give account of all his past life.
To prevent any divisions that might arise as to who should command, he asked that they be pleased to elect a principal and able
person to be governor, one with whom they should all be satisfied,
and, being chosen, they would swear before him to obey; that this
would greatly satisfy him, abate somewhat the pains he suffered,
and moderate the anxiety of leaving them in a country they knew
not where.

Baltasar de Gallegos responded in behalf of all. Thereupon the
Governor nominated Luys Moscoso de Alvarado to be his captain
general; when by all those present was he straightway chosen and
sworn Governor.

The next day, the 21st of May, departed this life the magnanimous,
the virtuous, the intrepid captain, Don Hernando de Soto, Governor
of Cuba and Adelantado of Florida. He was advanced by fortune
in the way she is wont to lead others, that he might fall the greater
depth; he died in a land, and at a time, that could afford him little
comfort in his illness. . . . Luys de Moscoso determined to conceal
what had happened from the Indians, for De Soto had given them to
understand that the Christians were immortal; besides, they held
him to be vigilant, sagacious, brave; and, although they were at
peace, should they know him to be dead, they, being of their nature
inconstant, might venture on making an attack. And they were
credulous of all that he had told them, for he made them believe
that some things which went on among them privately he had discovered without their being able to see how, or by what means;
and that the figure which appeared in a mirror he showed, told him
whatsoever they might be about, or desired to do; whence neither
by word nor deed did they dare undertake anything to his injury.

So soon as the death had taken place, Luys de Moscoso directed
the body to be put secretly into a house, where it remained three

days; and thence it was taken at night, by his order, to a gate of the town, and buried within. The Indians who had seen him ill, finding him no longer, suspected the reason; and passing by where he lay, they observed the ground loose, and, looking about, talked among themselves. This coming to the knowledge of Luys de Moscoso, he ordered the corpse to be taken up at night, and among the shawls that enshrouded it having cast abundance of sand, it was taken out in a canoe and committed to the middle of the stream. The cacique of Guachoya asked for him, saying: "What has been done with my brother and lord, the Governor?" Luys de Moscoso told him that he had ascended into the skies, as he had done on many other occasions, but as he would have to be detained there some time, he had left him in his stead. The chief, thinking within himself that he was dead, ordered two well-proportioned young men to be brought, saying that it was the usage of the country when any lord died to kill some persons, who should accompany and serve him on the way, on which account they were brought; and he told him to command their heads to be struck off that they might go accordingly to attend his friend and master. Luys de Moscoso replied to him that the Governor was not dead, but only gone into the heavens, having taken with him of his soldiers sufficient number for his need.

Narrative of the Expedition of Hernando de Soto
by the Gentleman of Elvas

# 4. Marquette and Joliet Float down the Mississippi

*As De Soto represented the southern incursion into what is now the United States, so Marquette represented the incursion from the north. He was, of course, not the first great French explorer of North America. Cartier, Champlain, and Jean Nicolet had all preceded him. But he, La Salle, and Joliet were the first to push past the hostile Iroquois and penetrate to the very heart of present-day America; they were the men who laid the foundation of French hopes of a great empire in the Mississippi Valley. Father Jacques Marquette, who was not quite thirty when he reached Canada in 1666 as a Jesuit missionary, was sent two years later to the upper lakes of the St. Lawrence. Then in 1673 he was chosen with Joliet to explore the Mississippi, of which stories had reached the French from the prairie tribes. The two heroic men descended the river as far as the mouth of the Arkansas before they turned back.*

ON THE 17th day of May, 1673, we started from the mission of St. Ignatius at Michilimakinac, where I then was. The joy that we felt at being selected for this expedition animated our courage and rendered the labor of paddling from morning to night agreeable to us. And because we were going to seek unknown countries, we took every precaution in our power, so that, if our undertaking were hazardous, it should not be foolhardy. To that end we obtained all the information that we could from the savages who had frequented those regions; and we even traced out from their reports a map of the whole of that new country; on it we indicated the rivers which we were to navigate, the names of the people and of the places through which we were to pass, the course of the great river, and the direction we were to follow when we reached it.

With all these precautions, we joyfully plied our paddles on a portion of Lake Huron, on that of the Illinois, and on the Bay des Puants.

The first nation that we came to was that of the Folle Avoine [Menominee]. I entered their river to go and visit these peoples to whom we have preached the Gospel for several years — in consequence of which, there are several good Christians among them.

I told these people of the Folle Avoine of my design to go and discover those remote nations, in order to teach them the mysteries of our holy religion. They were greatly surprised to hear it, and did their best to dissuade me. They represented to me that I would meet nations who never show mercy to strangers, but break their heads without any cause; and that war was kindled between various peoples who dwelt upon our route, which exposed us to the further manifest danger of being killed by the bands of warriors who are ever in the field. They also said that the great river was very dangerous, when one does not know the difficult places; that it was full of horrible monsters, which devoured men and canoes together; that there was even a demon, who was heard from a great distance, who barred the way and swallowed up all who ventured to approach him; finally, that the heat was so excessive in those countries that it would inevitably cause our death.

I thanked them for the good advice that they gave me, but told them that I could not follow it, because the salvation of souls was at stake, for which I would be delighted to give my life; that I scoffed at the alleged demon; that we would easily defend ourselves against those marine monsters; and, moreover, that we would be on our guard to avoid the other dangers with which they threatened us. After making them pray to God, and giving them some instruction, I separated from them.

Here we are at Maskoutens. This word may, in Algonquin, mean "the Fire Nation" — which, indeed, is the name given to this tribe. Here is the limit of the discoveries which the French have made, for they have not yet gone any farther. . . .

No sooner had we arrived than we, Monsieur Joliet and I, assembled the elders together; and he told them that he was sent by Monsieur our Governor to discover new countries, while I was sent by God to illumine them with the light of the holy Gospel. He told them that, moreover, the Sovereign Master of our lives wished to be known by all the nations; and that in obeying His will I feared not the death to which I exposed myself in voyages so perilous. He informed them that we needed two guides to show us the way; and we gave them a present, by it asking them to grant us the guides. To this they very civilly consented; and they also spoke to us by means of a present, consisting of a mat to serve us as a bed during the whole of our voyage.

On the following day, the 10th of June, two Miamis who were given us as guides embarked with us, in the sight of a great crowd, who could not sufficiently express their astonishment at the sight

of seven Frenchmen, alone and in two canoes, daring to undertake so extraordinary and so hazardous an expedition.

We knew that, at three leagues from Maskoutens, was a river
which discharged into the Mississippi. We knew also that the direction we were to follow in order to reach it was west-southwesterly.
But the road is broken by so many swamps and small lakes that it
is easy to lose one's way, especially as the river leading thither
is so full of wild oats that it is difficult to find the channel. For this
reason we greatly needed our two guides, who safely conducted
us to a portage of twenty-seven hundred paces, and helped us to
transport our canoes to enter that river, after which they returned
home, leaving us alone in this unknown country, in the hands of
Providence.

Thus we left the waters flowing to Quebec, four or five hundred
leagues from here, to float on those that would thenceforward take
us through strange lands.

The river on which we embarked is called Wisconsin. It is very
wide; it has a sandy bottom, which forms various shoals that render
its navigation very difficult. It is full of islands covered with vines.
On the banks one sees fertile land, diversified with woods, prairies,
and hills. There are oak, walnut, and basswood trees, and another
kind whose branches are armed with long thorns. We saw there
neither feathered game nor fish, but many deer, and a large number of cattle. Our route lay to the southwest, and after navigating
about thirty leagues we saw a spot presenting all the appearances
of an iron mine; and, in fact, one of our party who had formerly
seen such mines assures us that the one which we found is very
good and very rich. It is covered with three feet of good soil and is
quite near a chain of rocks, the base of which is covered by very
fine trees. After proceeding forty leagues on this same route, we arrived at the mouth of our river; and, at forty-two and a half degrees of latitude, we safely entered the Mississippi on the 17th of
June, with a joy that I cannot express.

Here we are then, on this so renowned river, all of whose peculiar features I have endeavored to note carefully. The Mississippi
takes its rise in various lakes in the country of the northern nations. It is narrow at the place where Miskous [the Wisconsin] emp-

ties; its current, which flows southward, is slow and gentle. To the right is a large chain of very high mountains, and to the left are beautiful lands; in various places the stream is divided by islands. From time to time, we came upon monstrous fish, one of which struck our canoe with such violence that I thought that it was a great tree about to break the canoe to pieces. On another occasion, we saw on the water a monster with the head of a tiger, a sharp nose like that of a wildcat, with whiskers and straight, erect ears; the head was gray and the neck quite black; but we saw no more creatures of this sort. When we cast our nets into the water we caught sturgeon, and a very extraordinary kind of fish. It resembles the trout, with this difference, that its mouth is larger. Near its nose — which is smaller, as are also the eyes — is a large bone, shaped like a woman's busk, three fingers wide and a cubit long, at the end of which is a disk as wide as one's hand. This frequently causes it to fall backward when it leaps out of the water. When we reached the parallel of forty-one degrees, twenty-eight minutes, following the same direction, we found that turkeys had taken the place of game; and the pisikious, or wild cattle [buffalo], that of the other animals.

We continued to advance, but, as we knew not whither we were going — for we had proceeded over one hundred leagues without discovering anything except animals and birds — we kept well on our guard. On this account, we make only a small fire on land, toward evening, to cook our meals; and, after supper, we remove ourselves as far from it as possible, and pass the night in our canoes, which we anchor in the river at some distance from the shore. This does not prevent us from always posting one of the party as a sentinel for fear of a surprise. Proceeding still in a southerly and south-southwesterly direction, we find ourselves at the parallel of forty-one degrees, and as low as forty degrees and some minutes — partly southeast and partly southwest — after having advanced over sixty leagues since we entered the river, without discovering anything.

Finally on the 25th of June we perceived on the water's edge some tracks of men, and a narrow and somewhat beaten path leading to a fine prairie. We stopped to examine it; and, thinking that it was a road which led to some village of savages, we resolved to go and reconnoiter it. We therefore left our two canoes under the guard of our people, strictly charging them not to allow themselves to be surprised, after which Monsieur Joliet and I undertook this investigation — a rather hazardous one for two men who exposed themselves alone to the mercy of a barbarous and unknown people. We silently followed the narrow path, and, after walking about two leagues, we discovered a village on the bank of a river, and two others on a hill distant about half a league from the first. Then we heartily commended ourselves to God, and, after imploring His aid, we went farther without being perceived, and approached so near that we could even hear the savages talking. We therefore decided that it was time to reveal ourselves. This we did by shouting with all our energy, and stopped without advancing any farther. On hearing the shout, the savages quickly issued from their cabins, and having probably recognized us as Frenchmen, especially when they saw a black gown — or, at least, having no cause for distrust, as we were only two men, and had given them notice of our arrival — they deputed four old men to come and speak to us. Two of these bore tobacco pipes, finely ornamented and adorned with various feathers. They walked slowly, and raised their pipes toward the sun, seemingly offering them to it to smoke — without, however, saying a word. They spent a rather long time in covering the short distance between their village and us. Finally, when they had drawn near, they stopped to consider us attentively. I was reassured when I observed these ceremonies, which with them are performed only among friends; and much more so when I saw them clad in cloth, for I judged thereby that they were our allies. I therefore spoke to them first, and asked who they were. They replied that they were Illinois; and, as a token of peace, they offered us their pipes to smoke. They afterward invited us to enter their village, where all the people impatiently awaited us.

The Jesuit Relations, Vol. LIX

# II

## Planting Colonies in the
## New World

Attributed to Albert Cuyp, 1620-1691

Pilgrims About to Go on Board the *Speedwell*

# 5. John Smith Founds Jamestown and Is Saved by Pocahontas

*The nation that was to give its language and civilization to most of North America planted its first permanent settlement in Virginia under a company of gentlemen and merchants, the Virginia Company, which John Smith claimed to have been largely instrumental in promoting. He was a figure worthy of the English race which found in him its first great American representative: intrepid before danger, stubbornly indomitable under hardship, resourceful in emergencies, full of energy, zest, and enterprise. As 1606 drew to a close he and 143 other colonists sailed from London with their orders sealed in a box; the following May they disembarked 105 strong at Jamestown. Smith was one of the council of seven appointed to administer the colony during its first year, and was worth all the others put together. Some of his stories may have grown in the telling, though even the Pocahontas episode has no inherent improbability; but that his exertions in getting food from the Indians saved the starving settlers, that his other measures showed admirable judgment, there can be no doubt. His brief career in Virginia was not more important than the contributions he made toward the founding of New England, but it is so spectacular that the American imagination has never tired of dwelling upon it.*

## I

AFTER many crosses in The Downs by tempests, we arrived safely upon the southwest part of the great Canaries; within four or five days after we set sail for Dominica, the 26th of April [1607]. The first land we made, we fell with Cape Henry, the very mouth of the Bay of Chesapeake, which at that present we little expected, having by a cruel storm been put to the northward. Anchoring in this bay, twenty or thirty went ashore with the Captain, and in coming aboard they were assaulted with certain Indians which charged them within pistolshot, in which conflict Captain Archer and Mathew Morton were shot. Whereupon Captain Newport, seconding them, made a shot at them which the Indians little respected, but having spent their arrows retired without harm. And in that place was the box opened wherein the Council for Virginia was nominated. And arriving at the place where we are now seated, the Council was sworn and the president elected . . . where was made choice for our situation a very fit place for the erecting of a great city. All our provision was brought ashore, and with as much speed as might be we went about our fortification. . . .

Captain Newport, having set things in order, set sail for England the 22d of June, leaving provision for thirteen or fourteen weeks. The day before the ship's departure, the king of Pamaunkee sent the Indian that had met us before, in our discovery, to assure us of peace. Our fort being then palisaded round, and all our men in good health and comfort, albeit that through some discontented humors it did not so long continue. God (being angry with us) plagued us with such famine and sickness that the living were scarce able to bury the dead — our want of sufficient and good victuals, with continual watching, four or five each night at three bulwarks, being the chief cause. Only of sturgeon had we great store, whereon our men would so greedily surfeit as it cost many lives. . . . Shortly after it pleased God, in our extremity, to move the Indians to bring us corn, ere it was half ripe, to refresh us when we rather expected they would destroy us. About the 10th of September there were about forty-six of our men dead. . . .

Our provisions being now within twenty days spent, the Indians brought us great store both of corn and bread ready-made, and also there came such abundance of fowls into the rivers as greatly refreshed our weak estates, whereupon many of our weak men were presently able to go abroad. As yet we had no houses to cover us, our tents were rotten, and our cabins worse than nought. Our best commodity was iron, which we made into little chisels. The president and Captain Martin's sickness constrained me to

be cape merchant, and yet to spare no pains in making houses for
the company, who, notwithstanding our misery, little ceased their
malice, grudging and muttering.

As at this time most of our chiefest men were either sick or discontented, the rest being in such despair as they would rather
starve and rot with idleness than be persuaded to do anything for
their own relief without constraint, our victuals being now within
eighteen days spent, and the Indian trade decreasing, I was sent
to the mouth of the river, to Kegquouhtan and Indian town, to
trade for corn and try the river for fish; but our fishing we could
not effect by reason of the stormy weather. With fish, oysters, bread,
and deer they kindly traded with me and my men.

JOHN SMITH, A True Relation

## II

And now [1608], the winter approaching, the rivers became so
covered with swans, geese, ducks, and cranes, that we daily feasted
with good bread, Virginia peas, pumpkins, and putchamins, fish,
fowl, and divers sorts of wild beasts as fat as we could eat them: so
that none of our tuftaffety humorists desired to go for England.

But our comedies never endured long without a tragedy; some
idle exceptions being muttered against Captain Smith for not discovering the head of Chickahamania River, and taxed by the Council
to be too slow in so worthy an attempt. The next voyage he proceeded so far that with much labor by cutting of trees asunder he
made his passage; but when his barge could pass no farther, he
left her in a broad bay out of danger of shot, commanding none
should go ashore till his return: himself with two English and two
savages went up higher in a canoe; but he was not long absent but
his men went ashore, whose want of government gave both occasion and opportunity to the savages to surprise one George Cassen,
whom they slew, and much failed not to have cut off the boat and
all the rest.

Smith, little dreaming of that accident, being got to the marshes
at the river's head, twenty miles in the desert, had his two men
slain, as is supposed, sleeping by the canoe, whilst himself by
fowling sought them victual: finding he was beset with 200 sav-

ages, two of them he slew, still defending himself with the aid of a savage his guide, whom he bound to his arm with his garters, and used him as a buckler, yet he was shot in his thigh a little, and had many arrows that stuck in his clothes; but no great hurt, till at last they took him prisoner. When this news came to Jamestown, much was their sorrow for his loss, few expecting what ensued.

Six or seven weeks those barbarians kept him prisoner, many strange triumphs and conjurations they made of him, yet he so demeaned himself amongst them, as he not only diverted them from surprising the fort but procured his own liberty, and got himself and his company such estimation amongst them that those savages admired him more than their own Quiyouckosucks.

The manner how they used and delivered him is as follows. . . .

He demanding for their captain, they showed him Opechan-kanough, king of Pamaunkee, to whom he gave a round ivory double compass dial. Much they marveled at the playing of the fly and needle, which they could see so plainly and yet not touch it because of the glass that covered them. But when he demonstrated by that globe-like jewel the roundness of the earth and skies, the sphere of the sun, moon, and stars, and how the sun did chase the night round about the world continually; the greatness of the land and sea, the diversity of nations, variety of complexions, and how we were to them antipodes, and many other such like matters, they all stood as amazed with admiration. Notwithstanding, within an hour after they tied him to a tree, and as many as could stand about him prepared to shoot him: but the king holding up the compass in his hand, they all laid down their bows and arrows, and in a triumphant manner led him to Orapaks, where he was after their manner kindly feasted, and well used.

At last they brought him to Werowocomoco, where was Pow-hatan, their emperor. Here more than two hundred of those grim courtiers stood wondering at him, as he had been a monster; till Powhatan and his train had put themselves in their greatest braveries. Before a fire upon a seat like a bedstead, he sat covered with a great robe, made of raccoon skins, and all the tails hanging by. On either hand did sit a young wench of sixteen or eighteen years, and along on each side the house, two rows of men, and behind them as many women, with all their heads and shoulders painted red, many of their heads bedecked with the white down of birds, but every one with something, and a great chain of white beads about their necks. At his entrance before the king, all the people gave a great shout. The queen of Appamatuck was appointed to bring him water to wash his hands, and another brought him a bunch of feathers, instead of a towel to dry them. Having feasted him after their best barbarous manner they could, a long consultation was held, but the conclusion was, two great stones were brought before Powhatan: then as many as could laid hands on him, dragged him to them, and thereon laid his head, and being ready with their clubs to beat out his brains, Pocahontas, the king's dearest daughter, when no entreaty could prevail, got his head in her arms, and laid her own upon his to save his from death: whereat the emperor was contented he should live to make him hatchets, and her bells, beads, and copper; for they thought him as well of all occupations as themselves. For the king himself will make his own robes, shoes, bows, arrows, pots; plant, hunt, or do anything so well as the rest.

Two days after, Powhatan having disguised himself in the most fearfulest manner he could, caused Captain Smith to be brought forth to a great house in the woods, and there upon a mat by the fire to be left alone. Not long after, from behind a mat that divided the house was made the most dolefulest noise he ever heard; then Powhatan, more like a devil than a man, with some two hundred more as black as himself, came unto him and told him now they were friends, and presently he should go to Jamestown, to send him two great guns, and a grindstone, for which he would give him the county of Capahowosick, and for ever esteem him as his son Nantaquoud.

JOHN SMITH, The Generall Historie of Virginia

# 6. The Pilgrims Arrive Safely at Plymouth

*The Pilgrims in the* Mayflower, *like John Smith's fellow settlers at Jamestown, were the pioneers of a mighty host; and we know now that the two great streams of migration, that to Massachusetts and that to Virginia, were not so unlike as was long supposed. Yet the Pilgrims and the Puritans did have some special characteristics. King James I yearned toward absolute sovereignty. He objected vigorously to the sect of Separatists who denied the supremacy of the crown over church affairs and demanded the right to organize their own congregations under their own ministers, without regard to king or bishop. "I will make them conform," exclaimed James at the Hampton Court conference, "or I will harry them out of the land." Leave the land, the Separatists or Congregationalists of Scrooby did, going first to Holland in 1607–1608, and then in 1617 deciding to found a Puritan state in America. Three years later an advance guard of the Leyden congregation left Delfthaven in the* Speedwell, *to be joined at Southampton by friends from London in the* Mayflower. *But the former boat leaked and it was the* Mayflower *alone that sailed from Plymouth in Devon on September 6, 1620, with about a hundred people aboard. This little handful had a religious fervor, a high-minded idealism, and an iron strength of character which left a clear impress on the nation they helped to found.*

## THEIR REMOVAL TO LEYDEN

FOR THESE and some other reasons they removed to Leyden, a fair and beautiful city, and of a sweet situation, but made more famous by the university wherewith it is adorned, in which of late had been so many learned men. But wanting that traffic by sea which Amsterdam enjoys, it was not so beneficial for their outward means of living and estates. But being now here pitched they fell to such trades and employments as they best could, valuing peace and their spiritual comfort above any other riches whatsoever. And at length they came to raise a competent and comfortable living but with hard and continual labor. . . .

## SHOWING THE REASONS AND CAUSES OF THEIR REMOVAL

After they had lived in this city about some eleven or twelve years, and sundry of them were taken away by death and many others began to be well stricken in years, the grave mistress Experience having taught them many things, those prudent governors, with sundry of the sagest members, began both deeply to apprehend their present dangers and wisely to foresee the future and think of timely remedy. In the agitation of their thoughts and much discourse of things hereabout, at length they began to incline to this conclusion, of removal to some other place — not out of any new-fangledness or other such like giddy humor by which men are oftentimes transported to their great hurt and danger, but for sundry weighty and solid reasons, some of the chief of which I will here briefly touch. And first, they saw and found by experience the hardness of the place and country to be such as few in comparison would come to them, and fewer that would bide it out, and continue with them. For many that came to them and many more that desired to be with them could not endure that great labor and hard fare, with other inconveniences which they underwent and were contented with.

Secondly, they saw that though the people generally bore all these difficulties very cheerfully and with a resolute courage, being in the best and strength of their years, yet old age began to steal on many of them (and their great and continual labors, with other crosses and sorrows, hastened it before the time), so as it was not only probably thought, but apparently seen, that within a few years more they would be in danger to scatter, by necessities pressing them, or sink under their burdens, or both.

Thirdly, as necessity was a taskmaster over them, so they were forced to be such, not only to their servants but in a sort to their dearest children; the which as it did not a little wound the tender hearts of many a loving father and mother, so it produced likewise sundry sad and sorrowful effects. But that which was more lamentable, and, of all sorrows, most heavy to be borne, was that many of their children, by these occasions and the great licentiousness of youth in that country, and the manifold temptations of the place, were drawn away by evil examples into extravagant and dangerous courses, getting the reins of their necks and departing from their parents. Some became soldiers, others took upon them far voyages by sea, and others some worse courses, tending to dissoluteness and the danger of their souls, to the great grief of their parents and dishonor of God. So that they saw their posterity would be in danger to degenerate and be corrupted.

Lastly (and which was not least), a great hope and inward zeal they had of laying some good foundation, or at least to make some way thereunto, for the propagating and advancing the gospel of the kingdom of Christ in those remote parts of the world; yea, though they should be but even as stepping-stones unto others for the performing of so great a work.

The place they had thoughts on was some of those vast and unpeopled countries of America, which are fruitful and fit for habitation, being devoid of all civil inhabitants, where there are only savage and brutish men, which range up and down, little otherwise than the wild beasts of the same. This proposition being made public and coming to the scanning of all, it raised many variable opinions amongst men, and caused many fears and doubts amongst themselves. Some, from their reasons and hopes conceived, labored to stir up and encourage the rest to undertake and prosecute the same; others, again, out of their fears, objected against it and sought to divert from it, alleging many things, and those neither unreasonable nor unprobable, as that it was a great design and subject to many unconceivable perils and dangers; as, besides the casualties of the seas (which none can be freed from) the length of the voyage was such as the weak bodies of women and other persons worn out with age and travel (as many of them were) could never be able to endure. And yet if they should, the miseries of the land which they should be exposed unto would be too hard to be borne, and likely, some or all of them together, to consume and utterly to ruinate them. For there they should be liable to famine, and nakedness, and the want, in a manner, of all things. The change of air, diet, and drinking of water, would infect their bodies with sore sicknesses and grievous diseases. And also those which should escape or overcome these difficulties should yet be in continual danger of the savage people, who are cruel, barbarous, and most treacherous, being most furious in their rage, and merciless where they overcome, not being content only to kill and take away life, but delight to torment men in the most bloody manner that may be, flaying some alive with the shells of fishes, cutting off the members and joints of others by piecemeal, and broiling on the coals, eat the collops of their flesh in their sight whilst they live; with other cruelties horrible to be related. And surely it could not be thought but the very hearing of these things could not but move the very bowels of men to grate within them, and make the weak to quake and tremble. It was further objected that it would require greater sums of money to furnish such a voyage and to fit them with necessaries than their consumed estates would amount to; and yet they must as well look to be seconded with supplies as presently to be transported. Also many precedents of ill success and lamentable miseries befallen others in the like designs were easy to be found, and not forgotten to be alleged; besides their own experience, in their former troubles and hardships in their removal into Holland, and how hard a thing it was for them to live in that strange place, though it was a neighbor country and a civil and rich commonwealth.

It was answered that all great and honorable actions are accompanied with great difficulties, and must be both enterprised and overcome with answerable courages. It was granted the dangers were great but not desperate; the difficulties were many but not invincible. For though there were many of them likely, yet they were not certain; it might be sundry of the things feared might never befall; others, by provident care and the use of good means, might in a great measure be prevented; and all of them, through the help of God, by fortitude and patience, might either be borne or overcome. True it was that such attempts were not to be made and undertaken without good ground and reason, not rashly or lightly, as many have done for curiosity or hope of gain, etc. But their condition was not ordinary; their ends were good and honorable, their calling lawful and urgent; and therefore they might expect the blessing of God in their proceeding. Yea, though they should lose their lives in this action, yet might they have comfort in the same, and their endeavors would be honorable. . . . After many other particular things answered and alleged on both sides, it was fully concluded by the major part to put this design in execution and to prosecute it by the best means they could.

## OF THEIR DEPARTURE FROM LEYDEN, WITH THEIR ARRIVAL AT SOUTHAMPTON

At length, after much travel and these debates, all things were got ready and provided. A small ship was bought and fitted in Holland, which was intended as to serve to help to transport them so to stay in the country and attend upon fishing and such other affairs as might be for the good and benefit of the colony when they came there. Another was hired at London, of burden about ninescore, and all other things got in readiness. So, being ready to depart, they had a day of solemn humiliation, their pastor taking his text from Ezra viii, 21. *And there at the river, by Ahava, I proclaimed a fast, that we might humble ourselves before our God, and seek of him a right way for us, and for our children, and for all our substance.* Upon which he spent a good part of the day very profitably, and suitable to their present occasion. The rest of the time was spent in pouring out prayers to the Lord with great fervency mixed with abundance of tears. And the time being come that they must depart, they were accompanied with most of their brethren out of the city unto a town sundry miles off called Delfthaven, where the ship lay ready to receive them. So they left the goodly and pleasant city which had been their resting place near twelve years; but they knew they were pilgrims and looked not much on those things but lifted up their eyes to the heavens, their dearest country, and quieted their spirits. When they came to the place they found the ship and all things ready; and such of their friends as could not come with them followed after them, and sundry also came from Amsterdam, to see them shipped and to take their leave of them. That night was spent with little sleep by the most, but with friendly entertainment and Christian discourse and other real expressions of true Christian love. The next day, the wind being fair, they went aboard, and their friends with them, where truly doleful was the sight of that sad and mournful parting; to see what sighs and sobs and prayers did sound amongst them, what tears did gush from every eye, and pithy speeches pierced each heart, that sundry of the Dutch strangers that stood on the quay as spectators could not refrain from tears. Yet comfortable and sweet it was to see such lively and true expressions of dear and unfeigned love. But the tide (which stays for no man) calling them away that were thus loath to depart, their reverend pastor, falling down on his knees (and they all with him), with watery cheeks commended them with most fervent prayers to the Lord and His blessing. And then with mutual embraces and many tears they took their leaves one of another, which proved to be the last leave to many of them. . . .

Being thus arrived in a good harbor and brought safe to land, they fell upon their knees and blessed the God of Heaven who had brought them over the vast and furious ocean and delivered them from all the perils and miseries thereof, again to set their feet on the firm and stable earth, their proper element.

But here I cannot but stay and make a pause and stand half amazed at this poor people's present condition; and so I think will the reader too, when he well considers the same. Being thus past the vast ocean and a sea of troubles before in their preparation (as may be remembered by that which went before), they had now no friends to welcome them, nor inns to entertain or refresh their weatherbeaten bodies, no houses or much less towns to repair to, to seek for succor. It is recorded in Scripture as a mercy to the apostle and his shipwrecked company, the barbarians showed them no small kindness in refreshing them, but these savage barbarians, when they met with them (as after will appear) were readier to fill their sides full of arrows than otherwise. And for the season, it was winter, and they that know the winters of that country know them to be sharp and violent and subject to cruel and fierce storms, dangerous to travel to known places, much more to search an unknown coast. Besides, what could they see but a hideous and desolate wilderness full of wild beasts and wild men? And what multitudes there might be of them they knew not. If it be said they had a ship to succor them, it is true; but what heard they daily from the master and company but that with speed they should look out a place with their shallop where they would be at some near distance; for the season was such as he would not stir from thence till a safe harbor was discovered by them where they would be and he might go without danger; and that victuals consumed apace but he must and would keep sufficient for themselves and their return. Yea, it was muttered by some that if they got not a place in time they would turn them and their goods ashore and leave them. Let it also be considered what weak hopes of supply and succor they left behind them that might bear up their minds in this sad condition and trials they were under; and they could not but be very small. It is true, indeed, the affections and love of their brethren at Leyden was cordial and entire towards them, but they had little power to help them or themselves; and how the case stood between them and the merchants at their coming away hath already been declared. What could now sustain them but the spirit of God and His grace? May not and ought not the children of these fathers rightly say: *Our fathers were Englishmen which came over this great ocean, and were ready to perish in this wilderness; but they cried unto the Lord, and he heard their voice and looked on their adversity, etc. Let them therefore praise the Lord, because he is good and his mercies endure forever. Yea, let them which have been redeemed of the Lord show how he hath delivered them from the hand of the oppressor. When they wandered in the desert wilderness out of the way, and found no city to dwell in, both hungry and thirsty, their soul was overwhelmed in them. Let them confess before the Lord his loving kindness, and his wonderful works before the sons of men.*

WILLIAM BRADFORD, History of Plimoth Plantation

# 7. Richard Mather Sails to Cape Cod

*After the Pilgrims, came the great Puritan exodus which within twenty years gave New England a population of 26,000 people. It was caused by the rise of the Stuart despotism in England, and ended by its fall — that is, by the meeting of the Long Parliament in 1640 to place sharp curbs upon Charles I. This exodus sent to America not only much the largest European*

*population which either continent had yet received, but a population
of remarkable qualities. It was purely and exclusively English; it was
profoundly religious; it was deeply attached to the idea of democratic
self-government; it was hardy, energetic, highly intelligent, and re-
markably prolific. In short, better seed for a new land could not have
been found. Typical of their fine qualities and also of their dogma-
tism was Richard Mather, founder of a famous American family,
who went to Brasenose at Oxford, took Anglican orders, turned to
Puritanism, and in 1635 sailed from Bristol to Massachusetts, where
he became minister of the church at Dorchester.*

WE CAME from Warrington on Thursday, April 16 [1635],
and came to Bristol on the Thursday following, viz. April 23, and
had a very healthful, safe, and prosperous journey all the way, blessed
be the name of God for the same, taking but easy journeys because
of the children and footmen, displacing one hundred and nineteen
or one hundred and twenty miles in seven days. . . .

Nevertheless we went not aboard the ship until Saturday, the
23d of May, so that the time of our staying in Bristol was a month
and two days, during all which time we found friendship and
courtesy at the hands of divers godly Christians in Bristol. Yet our
stay was grievous unto us when we considered how most of this time
the winds were easterly and served directly for us. But our ship was
not ready, so ill did our owners deal with us.

Going aboard the ship in King Road the 23d of May, we found
things very unready, and all on heaps, many goods being not stowed
but lying on disordered heaps here and there in the ship. This day
there came aboard the ship two of the searchers and viewed a list of
all our names, ministered the oath of allegiance to all at full age,
viewed our certificates from the ministers in the parishes from
whence we came, approved well thereof, and gave us tickets — that
is, licenses under their hands and seals, to pass the seas — and cleared
the ship, and so departed.

Thursday morning [May 28], the wind serving for us, and our
master and all the sailors being come aboard, we set sail and began
our sea voyage with glad hearts that God had loosed us from our

long stay wherein we had been holden, and with hope and trust that He would graciously guide us to the end of our journey. We were, that set sail together that morning, five ships: three bound for Newfoundland, viz. the *Diligence,* a ship of one hundred and fifty ton; the *Mary,* a small ship of eighty ton, and the *Bess;* and two bound for New England, viz. the *Angel Gabriel* of two hundred and forty ton, the *James* of two hundred and twenty ton.

Monday morning [June 22], the wind serving with a strong gale at east, we set sail from Milford Haven where we had waited for wind twelve days, and were carried forth with speedy course, and about noon lost all sight of land. The wind being strong, the sea was rough this day, and most of our passengers were very sick and ill through much casting.

Tuesday, the wind still easterly, and a very rainy day. We were carried forward apace and launched forth a great way into the deep, but our people were still very sick. This day at evening we lost sight of the three ships bound for Newfoundland, which had been in company with us from King Road.

Thursday morning [July 23], a fine gale of wind at north and by east. Now we saw this morning abundance of porpoises and grampuses, leaping and spewing up water about the ship. About eight or nine ot the clock the wind blew more stiffly and we went about eight or nine leagues a watch. Toward evening our seamen deemed that we were near to some land, because the color of the water was changed, but sounding with a line of an hundred and sixty fathom, they could find no bottom. It was a very cold wind, like as if it had been winter, which made some to wish for more clothes.

Friday, wind still northerly, but very faint. It was a great foggy mist, and exceeding cold as it had been December. One would have wondered to have seen the innumerable numbers of fowl which we saw swimming on every side of the ship, and mighty fishes rolling and tumbling in the waters, twice as long and big as an ox. In the afternoon we saw mighty whales spewing up water in the air like the smoke of a chimney, and making the sea about them white and hoary.

[July 26.] The fifth Sabbath from Milford Haven and the tenth on shipboard; a fair sunshiny summer day, and would have been very hot, had not God allayed the heat with a good gale of southerly wind, by which also we were carried on in our journey after seven leagues a watch. I was exercised [preached] in the forenoon and Mr. Maude in the afternoon. In the afternoon the wind grew stronger, and it was a rough night for wind and rain, and some had our beds that night ill wet with rain leaking in through the sides of the ship.

Monday [July 27], wind still strong at south. This day we spent much time in filling divers tuns of emptied cask with salt water; which was needful, because much beer, fresh water, beef, and other provisions being spent, the ship went not so well, being too light for want of ballast. When this work was done we set forth more sail, and went that evening and all the night following with good speed in our journey.

Tuesday morning, a great calm, and very hot all that forenoon; our people and cattle being much afflicted with faintness, sweating, and heat; but (lo the goodness of our God) about noon the wind blew at north and by east, which called us from our heat and helped us forward in our way. This afternoon there came and lit upon our ship a little land bird with blue-colored feathers, about the bigness of a sparrow, by which some conceived we were not far from land.

Thursday, wind still westerly against us all the forenoon, but about one of the clock the Lord remembered us in mercy, and sent us a fresh gale at south; which though weak and soft yet did not only much mitigate the heat, but also helped us something forward in our way. In the evening about sunsetting, we saw with admiration and delight innumerable multitudes of huge grampuses rolling and tumbling about the sides of the ship, spewing and puffing up water as they went, and pursuing great numbers of bonitos and lesser fishes; so marvelous to behold are the works and wonders of the Almighty in the deep.

Saturday morning [August 1], a cool wind at north, whereby we went on in our course an hour or two, though very slowly because of the weakness of the wind. Afterwards it became a great calm; and our seamen sounded about one of the clock and found ground at sixty fathom. Presently after, another little land bird came and lit upon the sails of the ship. In the cool of the evening (the calm still continuing) our seamen fished with hook and line and took cod as fast as they could haul them up into the ship.

[August 3.] But lest we should grow secure and neglect the Lord through abundance of prosperity, our wise and loving God was pleased on Monday morning about three of the clock, when we were upon the coast of land, to exercise us with a sore storm and tempest of wind and rain; so that many of us passengers with wind and rain were raised out of our beds, and our seamen were forced to let down all the sails; and the ship was so tossed with fearful mountains and valleys of water, as if we should have been overwhelmed and swallowed up. But this lasted not long, for at our poor prayers the Lord was pleased to magnify His mercy in assuaging the winds and seas again about sunrising. But the wind was become west against us, so that we floated upon the coast, making no dispatch of way all that day and the night following; and besides there was a great fog and mist all that day, so that we could not see to make land, but kept in all sail, and lay still, rather losing than gaining, but taking abundance of cod and halibut, wherewith our bodies were abundantly refreshed after they had been tossed with the storm.

Tuesday, the fog still continued all forenoon; about noon the day cleared up, and the wind blew with a soft gale at south, and we set sail again, going on in our course, though very slowly because of the smallness of the wind. At night it was a calm and abundance of rain.

Saturday morning [August 8] we had a good gale of wind at westsouthwest; and this morning our seamen took abundance of mackerel, and about eight of the clock we all had a clear and comfortable sight of America and made land again at an island called Menhiggin, an island without inhabitants about thirty-nine leagues northward or northeast short of Cape Anne. A little from the island we saw more northward divers other islands called St. George Islands, and the mainland of New England all along northward and eastward as we sailed. This mercy of our God we had cause more highly to esteem of, because when we first saw land this morning there was a great fog; and afterward when the day cleared up we saw many rocks and islands almost on every side of us, as Menhiggin, St. George Islands, Pemmequid, etc. Yet in the midst of these dangers our God preserved us, though, because of the thick fog we could not see far about us to look unto ourselves. In the afternoon, the wind continuing still westward against us, we lay off again to the sea southward, and our seamen and many passengers delighted themselves in taking abundance of mackerel.

Wednesday morning [August 12], the wind serving with a fresh gale at north and by east, we set sail from Richmond's Island for Massachusetts Bay, and went along the coast by Cape Porpoise still within sight of land. This day the wind was soft and gentle, and as we went along our seamen and passengers took abundance of mackerel. Towards night it became a calm, so that then we could dispatch little way.

[August 15.] But yet the Lord had not done with us, nor yet had let us see all His power and goodness which He would have us take knowledge of; and therefore on Saturday morning about break of day, the Lord sent forth a most terrible storm of rain and easterly wind, whereby we were in as much danger as I think ever people were, for we lost in that morning three great anchors and cables, of which cables one having cost fifty pounds never had been in any water before; two were broken by the violence of the waves, and the third cut by the seamen in extremity and distress to save the ship and their and our lives. And when our cables and anchors were all lost, we had no outward means of deliverance but by losing sail, if so be we might get to the sea from amongst the islands and rocks where we anchored. In this extremity and appearance of death, as distress and distraction would suffer us, we cried unto the Lord and He was pleased to have compassion and pity upon us; for by His overruling providence and His own immediate good hand, He guided the ship past the rock, assuaged the violence of the sea, and the wind and rain, and gave us a little respite to fit the ship with other sails.

This day [August 16] we went on towards Cape Anne, as the wind would suffer, and our poor sails further, and came within sight thereof the other morning, which Sabbath being the thirteenth we kept on shipboard was a marvelous pleasant day, for a fresh gale of wind and clear sunshine weather. This day we went directly before the wind and had delight all along the coast as we went, in

viewing Cape Anne, the bay of Saugus, the bay of Salem, Marble-
head, Pullin Point, and other places, and came to anchor at low tide
in the evening at Nantascot in a most pleasant harbor like to which
I had never seen, amongst a great many islands on every side. I
was exercised [preached] on shipboard both ends of the day. After
the evening's exercise, when it was flowing tide again, we set sail
and came that night to anchor again before Boston, and so rested
that night with glad and thankful hearts that God had put an end
to our long journey, being a thousand leagues, that is three thousand
miles English, over one of the greatest seas in the world.

Richard Mather's Journal

# 8. Wouter Van Twiller Rules in New Amsterdam

*While the English colonies in Virginia
and Massachusetts were growing sturdily, the Dutch were making
stormier, slower headway in New Amsterdam, where they had
planted their first party of permanent settlers in 1623. The Dutch
were in some respects good colonizers. But they never learned, as the
English did, to transfer self-government to the New World, and self-
government is indispensable to a vigorous community. Rulers like
Wouter Van Twiller, William Kieft, and Peter Stuyvesant tried to
keep an iron hand upon the conduct of affairs, and found themselves
involved in constant bickering. Of these three, Wouter — "Walter
the Doubter" — was the weakest. Yet Irving's portrait or, rather,
caricature of him unquestionably does some injustice to this ill-
educated Amsterdam clerk, promoted (chiefly by marriage) to be
governor of New Amsterdam; he had more sense and character
than the humorist indicates. But within limits, as John Fiske states,
Irving gives a correct impression of the burly Dutchman's weak-
nesses. He came in 1633, and held office less than five years.*

IN THE year of our Lord 1629, Mynheer Wouter Van Twiller was appointed governor of the province of Nieuw Nederlandts, under the commission and control of their High Mightinesses the Lords States General of the United Netherlands, and the privileged West India Company.

This renowned old gentleman arrived at New Amsterdam in the merry month of June, the sweetest month in all the year; when Dan Apollo seems to dance up the transparent firmament — when the robin, the thrush, and a thousand other wanton songsters make the woods to resound with amorous ditties, and the luxurious little boblincoln revels among the clover blossoms of the meadows — all which happy coincidence persuaded the old dames of New Amsterdam, who were skilled in the art of foretelling events, that this was to be a happy and prosperous administration.

The renowned Wouter (or Walter) Van Twiller was descended from a long line of Dutch burgomasters who had successively dozed away their lives and grown fat upon the bench of magistracy in Rotterdam, and who had comported themselves with such singular wisdom and propriety that they were never either heard or talked of — which, next to being universally applauded, should be the object of ambition of all magistrates and rulers. There are two opposite ways by which some men make a figure in the world, one by talking faster than they think and the other by holding their tongues and not thinking at all. By the first, many a smatterer acquires the reputation of a man of quick parts; by the other, many a dunderpate, like the owl, the stupidest of birds, comes to be considered the very type of wisdom. This, by the way, is a casual remark, which I would not, for the universe, have it thought I apply to Governor Van Twiller. It is true he was a man shut up within himself like an oyster and rarely spoke except in monosyllables, but then it was allowed he seldom said a foolish thing. So invincible was his gravity that he was never known to laugh or even to smile through the whole course of a long and prosperous life. Nay, if a joke were uttered in his presence that set light-minded hearers in a roar, it was observed to throw him into a state of perplexity. Sometimes he would deign to inquire into the matter, and when, after much explanation, the joke was made as plain as a pikestaff, he would continue to smoke his pipe in silence, and at length, knocking out the ashes, would exclaim: "Well! I see nothing in all that to laugh about."

With all his reflective habits, he never made up his mind on a subject. His adherents accounted for this by the astonishing magnitude of his ideas. He conceived every subject on so grand a scale that he had not room in his head to turn it over and examine both sides of it. Certain it is that if any matter were propounded to him on which ordinary mortals would rashly determine at first glance, he would put on a vague, mysterious look; shake his capacious head; smoke some time in profound silence, and at length observe that he "had his doubts about the matter"; which gained him the reputation of a man slow of belief and not easily imposed upon. What is more, it gained him a lasting name: for to this habit of the mind has been attributed his surname of Twiller, which is said to be a corruption of the original Twijfler, or, in plain English, *Doubter*.

The person of this illustrious old gentleman was formed and proportioned as though it had been molded by the hands of some cunning Dutch statuary as a model of majesty and lordly grandeur. He was exactly five feet six inches in height, and six feet five inches in circumference. His head was a perfect sphere, and of such stupendous dimensions that Dame Nature, with all her sex's ingenuity, would have been puzzled to construct a neck capable of supporting it; wherefore she wisely declined the attempt, and settled it firmly on the top of his backbone just between the shoulders. His body was oblong and particularly capacious at bottom; which was wisely ordered by Providence, seeing that he was a man of sedentary habits, and very averse to the idle labor of walking. His legs were short, but sturdy in proportion to the weight they had to sustain; so that when erect he had not a little the appearance of a beer barrel on skids. His face, that infallible index of the mind, presented a vast expanse, unfurrowed by any of those lines and angles which disfigure the human countenance with what is termed expression. Two small gray eyes twinkled feebly in the midst like two stars of lesser magnitude in a hazy firmament, and his full-fed cheeks, which seemed to have taken toll of everything that went into his mouth, were curiously mottled and streaked with dusky red like a Spitzenberg apple.

His habits were as regular as his person. He daily took his four stated meals, appropriating exactly an hour to each; he smoked and doubted eight hours, and he slept the remaining twelve of the four-and-twenty. Such was the renowned Wouter Van Twiller — a true philosopher, for his mind was either elevated above, or tranquilly settled below, the cares and perplexities of this world. He had lived in it for years without feeling the least curiosity to know whether the sun revolved round it, or it round the sun; and he had watched for at least half a century the smoke curling from his pipe to the ceiling, without once troubling his head with any of those numerous theories by which a philosopher would have perplexed his brain in accounting for its rising above the surrounding atmosphere.

In his council he presided with great state and solemnity. He sat in a huge chair of solid oak, hewn in the celebrated forest of the Hague, fabricated by an experienced timberman of Amsterdam, and curiously carved about the arms and feet into exact imitations of gigantic eagle's claws. Instead of a scepter he swayed a long Turkish pipe, wrought with jasmin and amber, which had been presented to a stadtholder of Holland at the conclusion of a treaty with one of the petty Barbary powers. In this stately chair would he sit and this magnificent pipe would he smoke, shaking his right knee with a constant motion, and fixing his eye for hours together upon a little print of Amsterdam, which hung in a black frame against the opposite wall of the council chamber. Nay, it has even been said that when any deliberation of extraordinary length and intricacy was on the carpet, the renowned Wouter would shut his eyes for full two hours at a time that he might not be disturbed by external objects — and at such times the internal commotion of his mind was evinced by certain regular guttural sounds, which his admirers declared were merely the noise of conflict made by his contending doubts and opinions.

WASHINGTON IRVING, A History of New York

# III

## Life in the American Colonies

*From "A Popular History of the United States" by
William Cullen Bryant and Sydney Howard Gay*

Bacon's Rebellion

# 9. The Puritans Hunt Witches in Salem

*Few episodes in colonial history are more tragic than the witchcraft prosecutions of 1692 in Massachusetts. Altogether, nineteen men and women were executed by a special court set up by Sir William Phips, the charge being that they had conspired with the devil to bewitch their neighbors. Belief in witchcraft had for centuries been general among both Catholics and Protestants; in the previous three hundred years thousands of supposed witches and wizards had been executed in England, and tens of thousands in Europe as a whole. But the great delusion in Massachusetts came when liberal men elsewhere were shaking themselves free from this kind of superstition. Cotton Mather did much by his writings and preaching to create the atmosphere which made the Salem executions possible, and publicly defended some of the sentences. But it was not long before a sharp reaction in sentiment occurred, and the legislature decreed a public fast by way of penance for the wrong that had been done.*

## THE TRIAL OF MARTHA CARRIER

MARTHA CARRIER was indicted for the bewitching of certain persons, according to the form usual in such cases pleading not guilty to her indictment. There were first brought in a considerable number of the bewitched persons, who not only made the court sensible of an horrid witchcraft committed upon them, but also deposed that it was Martha Carrier or her shape that grievously tormented them by biting, pricking, pinching, and choking of them. It was further deposed that while this Carrier was on her examination before the magistrates, the poor people were so tortured that every one expected their death upon the very spot, but that upon the binding of Carrier they were eased. Moreover the look of Carrier then laid the afflicted people for dead; and her touch, if her eye at the same time were off them, raised them again. Which things were also now seen upon her trial. And it was testified that upon the mention of some having their necks twisted almost round by the shape of this Carrier, she replied: "It's no matter though their necks had been twisted quite off."

Before the trial of this prisoner several of her own children had frankly and fully confessed, not only that they were witches themselves, but that this their mother had made them so. This confession they made with great shows of repentance, and with much demonstration of truth. They related place, time, occasion; they gave an account of journeys, meetings, and mischiefs by them performed, and were very credible in what they said. Nevertheless, this evidence was not produced against the prisoner at the bar, inasmuch as there was other evidence enough to proceed upon.

Benjamin Abbot gave in his testimony that last March was a twelvemonth this Carrier was very angry with him upon laying out some land near her husband's. Her expressions in this anger were that she "would stick as close to Abbot as the bark stuck to the tree; and that he should repent of it afore seven years came to an end, so as Doctor Prescot should never cure him." These words were heard by others besides Abbot himself, who also heard her say she "would hold his nose as close to the grindstone as ever it was held since his name was Abbot." Presently after this he was taken with a swelling in his foot, and then with a pain in his side, and exceedingly tormented. It bred into a sore, which was lanced by Doctor Prescot, and several gallons of corruption ran out of it. For six weeks it continued very bad, and then another sore bred in his groin, which was also lanced by Doctor Prescot. Another sore then bred in his groin, which was likewise cut, and put him to very great misery. He was brought unto death's door, and so remained until Carrier was taken and carried away by the constable, from which very day he began to mend and so grew better every day, and is well ever since.

Sarah Abbot also, his wife, testified that her husband was not only all this while afflicted in his body, but also that strange, extraordinary, and unaccountable calamities befell his cattle, their death being such as they could guess at no natural reason for.

Allin Toothaker testified that Richard, the son of Martha Carrier, having some difference with him, pulled him down by the hair of the head. When he rose again he was going to strike at Richard Carrier, but fell down flat on his back to the ground and had not power to stir hand or foot, until he told Carrier he yielded; and then he saw the shape of Martha Carrier go off his breast.

This Toothaker had received a wound in the wars, and he now testified that Martha Carrier told him he should never be cured. Just afore the apprehending of Carrier, he could thrust a knitting needle into his wound, four inches deep; but presently after her being seized, he was thoroughly healed.

He further testified that when Carrier and he sometimes were at variance, she would clap her hands at him, and say he "should get nothing by it." Whereupon he several times lost his cattle by strange deaths, whereof no natural causes could be given.

One Foster, who confessed her own share in the witchcraft for which the prisoner stood indicted, affirmed that she had seen the prisoner at some of their witch meetings, and that it was this Carrier who persuaded her to be a witch. She confessed that the devil carried them on a pole to a witch meeting; but the pole broke, and she hanging about Carrier's neck, they both fell down, and she then received an hurt by the fall whereof she was not at this very time recovered.

One Lacy, who likewise confessed her share in this witchcraft, now testified that she and the prisoner were once bodily present at a witch meeting in Salem Village; and that she knew the prisoner to be a witch, and to have been at a diabolical sacrament, and that the prisoner was the undoing of her and her children, by enticing them into the snare of the devil.

Another Lacy, who also confessed her share in this witchcraft, now testified that the prisoner was at the witch meeting, in Salem Village, where they had bread and wine administered unto them.

In the time of this prisoner's trial, one Susanna Sheldon in open court had her hands unaccountably tied together with a wheel band, so fast that without cutting it could not be loosed. It was done by a specter, and the sufferer affirmed it was the prisoner's.

Memorandum. This rampant hag, Martha Carrier, was the person of whom the confessions of the witches, and of her own children among the rest, agreed that the devil had promised her she should be Queen of Hell.

COTTON MATHER, *The Wonders of the Invisible World*

## THE TRIAL OF GOODWIFE COREY

On Monday, the 21st of March, the magistrates of Salem appointed to come to examination of Goodwife Corey. And about twelve of the clock they went into the meeting house, which was thronged with spectators. Mr. Noyes began with a very pertinent and pathetic prayer, and Goodwife Corey being called to answer to what was alleged against her, she desired to go to prayer, which was much wondered at, in the presence of so many hundred people. The magistrates told her they would not admit it; they came not there to hear her pray, but to examine her in what was alleged against her. The worshipful Mr. Hathorne asked her why she afflicted those children. She said she did not afflict them. He asked her, "Who did then?" She said, "I do not know; how should I know?"

The number of the afflicted persons were about that time ten, viz. four married women: Mrs. Pope, Mrs. Putnam, Goodwife Bibber, and an ancient woman named Goodall; three maids: Mary Walcut, Mercy Lewes, at Thomas Putnam's, and a maid at Dr. Griggs's; there were three girls from nine to twelve years of age, each of them, or thereabouts, viz. Elizabeth Parris, Abigail Williams, and Ann Putnam.

These were most of them at Goodwife Corey's examination, and did vehemently accuse her in the assembly of afflicting them, by biting, pinching, strangling, etc.; and that they did in their fit see her likeness coming to them, and bringing a book to them. She said she had no book. They affirmed she had a yellow bird that used to suck betwixt her fingers; and being asked about it, if she had any familiar spirit that attended her, she said she had no familiarity with any such thing, she was a gospel woman, which title she called herself by. And the afflicted persons told her ah, she was a gospel witch. Ann Putnam did there affirm that one day when Lieutenant Fuller was at prayer at her father's house, she saw the shape of Goodwife Corey and she thought Goodwife N., praying at the same time to the Devil. She was not sure it was Goodwife N., she thought it was, but very sure she saw the shape of Goodwife Corey. The said Corey said they were poor, distracted children, and no heed to be given to what they said. Mr. Hathorne and Mr. Noyes replied it was the judgment of all present they were bewitched, and only she, the accused person, said they were distracted.

It was observed several times that if she did but bite her underlip in time of examination, the persons afflicted were bitten on their arms and wrists and produced the marks before the magistrates, ministers, and others. And being watched for that, if she did but pinch her fingers, or grasp one hand hard in another, they were pinched, and produced the marks before the magistrates and spectators. After that, it was observed that if she did but lean her breast against the seat in the meeting house (being the bar at which she stood), they were afflicted. Particularly Mrs. Pope complained of grievous torment in her bowels as if they were torn out. She vehemently accused said Corey as the instrument, and first threw her muff at her, but that not flying home, she got off her shoe, and hit Goodwife Corey on the head with it. After these postures were watched, if said Corey did but stir her feet, they were afflicted in their feet, and stamped fearfully. The afflicted persons asked her why she did not go to the company of witches which were before the meeting house mustering. Did she not hear the drum beat? They accused her of having familiarity with the Devil, in the time of examination, in the shape of a black man whispering in her ear; they affirmed that her yellow bird sucked betwixt her fingers in the assembly; and, order being given to see if there were any sign, the girl that saw it said it was too late now; she had removed a pin and put it on her head, which was found there sticking upright.

They told her she had covenanted with the Devil for ten years; six of them were gone, and four more to come. She was required by the magistrates to answer that question in the catechism, "How many persons be there in the Godhead?" She answered it but oddly, yet there was no great thing to be gathered from it; she denied all that was charged upon her, and said they could not prove her a witch. She was that afternoon committed to Salem prison; and after she was in custody, she did not so appear to them and afflict them as before.

DEODAT LAWSON, Brief and True Narrative

## THE EXECUTIONS

August 5 [1692]. — The court again sitting, six more were tried on the same account, viz., Mr. George Burroughs, sometime minister of Wells, John Procter and Elizabeth Procter, his wife, with John Willard of Salem village, George Jacobs, Senior of Salem, and Martha Carrier of Andover. These were all brought in guilty, and condemned, and were all executed August 19, except Procter's wife, who pleaded pregnancy.

Mr. Burroughs was carried in a cart with the others through the streets of Salem to execution. When he was upon the ladder he made a speech for the clearing of his innocency with such solemn and serious expressions as were to the admiration of all present. His prayer (which he concluded by repeating the Lord's Prayer) was so well worded and uttered with such composedness and such (at least seeming) fervency of spirit as was very affecting, and drew tears from many (so that it seemed to some that the spectators would hinder the execution). The accusers said the Black Man stood and dictated to him. As soon as he was turned off, Mr. Cotton Mather, being mounted upon a horse, addressed himself to the people, partly to declare that he was no ordained minister and partly to possess the people of his guilt, saying that the Devil has often been transformed into an angel of light. And this did somewhat appease the people, and the executions went on. When he was cut down, he was dragged by the halter to a hole, or grave, between the rocks, about two foot deep; his shirt and breeches being pulled off and an old pair of trousers of one executed put on his lower parts, he was so put in, together with Willard and Carrier, one of his hands and his chin and a foot of one of them being left uncovered.

John Procter and his wife being in prison, the sheriff came to his house and seized all the goods, provisions, and cattle that he could come at, and sold some of the cattle at half price, and killed others.

and put them up for the West Indies; threw out the beer out of a barrel, and carried away the barrel; emptied a pot of broth, and took away the pot, and left nothing in the house for the support of the children. No part of the said goods are known to be returned. Procter earnestly requested Mr. Noyes to pray with and for him, but it was wholly denied, because he would not own himself to be a witch.

ROBERT CALEF, More Wonders of the Invisible World

# 10. Nathaniel Bacon Rebels against Governor Berkeley

*No less a person than a cousin of Lord Bacon headed the first important American rebellion. Nathaniel Bacon was a highly educated man, trained at Cambridge University and Gray's Inn. Settling in Virginia and gaining a seat on the Council, he witnessed with growing irritation the wrongs under which the common people of the colony labored. The king had made lavish grants of land to favorites. Lord Berkeley, the royal governor, seemed to have set up a political machine which was managing affairs for the benefit of a special group. Small farmers and planters complained that taxation was excessive and unfairly distributed; frontiersmen believed that the government and the rich tidewater landholders were not doing enough to furnish protection against the Indians. In 1676 a new set of Indian outrages brought the popular discontent to a head, and the people turned to the impetuous Bacon — wrathful because the savages had slain his overseer — for leader. His aims were twofold: to teach the Indians an enduring lesson, and then to wring reforms from the governor and the tidewater interests.*

IN THESE frightful times the most exposed small families withdrew into our houses, which we fortified with palisades and redoubts; neighbors in bodies joined their labors from each plantation to others alternately, taking their arms into the fields, and setting sentinels; no man stirred out of door unarmed. Indians were ever and anon espied, three, four, five, or six in a party, lurking throughout the whole land, yet (what was remarkable) I rarely heard of any houses burnt, though abundance was forsaken, nor ever of any corn or tobacco cut up, or other injury done, besides murders, except the killing a very few cattle and swine.

Frequent complaints of bloodsheds were sent to Sir William Berkeley (then governor) from the heads of the rivers, which were as often answered with promises of assistance.

These at the heads of James and York Rivers (having now most people destroyed by the Indians' flight thither from Potomac) grew impatient at the many slaughters of their neighbors and rose for their own defense, who choosing Mr. Bacon for their leader sent oftentimes to the Governor, humbly beseeching a commission to go against those Indians at their own charge, which his Honor as often promised, but did not send. . . .

During these protractions and people often slain, most or all the officers, civil and military, with as many dwellers next the heads of the rivers as made up three hundred men, taking Mr. Bacon for their commander, met, and concerted together the danger of going without a commission on the one part, and the continual murders of their neighbors on the other part (not knowing whose or how many of their own turns might be next) and came to this resolution, viz., to prepare themselves with necessaries for a march, but interim to send again for a commission, which if could or could not be obtained by a certain day, they would proceed, commission or no commission.

This day lapsing and no commission come, they marched into the wilderness in quest of these Indians, after whom the Governor sent his proclamation, denouncing all rebels who should not return within a limited day, whereupon those of estates obeyed. But Mr. Bacon with fifty-seven men proceeded until their provisions were near spent, without finding enemies; when coming nigh a fort of friendly Indians, on the other side a branch of James River, they desired relief, offering payment, which these Indians kindly promised to help them with on the morrow, but put them off with promises until the third day, so as having then eaten their last morsels they could not return, but must have starved on the way homeward. And now 'twas suspected these Indians had received private messages from the Governor, and those to be the causes of these delusive procrastinations; whereupon the English waded shoulder-deep through that branch to the fort palisades, still entreating and tendering pay, for victuals; but that evening a shot from the place they left on the other side of that branch killed one of Mr. Bacon's men, which made them believe those in the fort had sent for other Indians to come behind them and cut them off.

Hereupon they fired the palisades, stormed and burnt the fort and cabins, and (with the loss of three English) slew one hundred and fifty Indians.

From hence they returned home, where writs were come up to elect members for an Assembly, when Mr. Bacon was unanimously chosen for one, who coming down the river was commanded by a ship with guns to come on board, where waited Major Hone, the high sheriff of Jamestown, ready to seize him, by whom he was carried down to the Governor and by him received with a surprising civility in the following words: "Mr. Bacon, have you forgot to be a gentleman?" "No, may it please your Honor," answered Mr. Bacon; then replied the Governor, "I'll take your parole," and gave him his liberty. . . . The morning I arrived to Jamestown, after a week's voyage, was welcomed with the strange acclamations of "All's over, Bacon is taken," having not heard at home of the southern commotions, other than rumors like idle tales, of one Bacon risen up in rebellion, nobody knew for what, concerning the Indians.

The next forenoon, the Assembly being met in a chamber over the general court and our speaker chosen, the Governor sent for us down, where his Honor with a pathetic emphasis made a short, abrupt speech wherein were these words:

"If they had killed my grandfather and grandmother, my father and mother and all my friends, yet if they had come to treat of peace, they ought to have gone in peace," and sat down; the two chief commanders at the forementioned siege, who slew the four Indian great men, being present and part of our Assembly.

The Governor stood up again and said: "If there be joy in the presence of the angels over one sinner that repenteth, there is joy now, for we have a penitent sinner come before us. Call Mr. Bacon." Then did Mr. Bacon upon one knee at the bar deliver a paper confessing his crimes, and begging pardon of G and the Governor; whereto (after a short pause) he answered, "God forgive you, I forgive you," thrice repeating the same words; when Colonel Cole (one of the Council) said, "And all that were with him?" "Yea," said the Governor, "and all that were with him," twenty or more persons being then in irons, who were taken coming down in the same and other vessels with Mr. Bacon.

The Governor had directed us to consider of means for security from the Indian insults and to defray the charge. Whilst some days passed in settling the quotas of men, arms and ammunition, provisions, etc. each county was to furnish, one morning early a bruit ran about the town, "Bacon is fled, Bacon is fled." Bacon was escaped into the country, having intimation that the Governor's generosity in pardoning him and his followers, and restoring him to his seat in Council, were no other than previous wheedles to amuse him and his adherents and to circumvent them by stratagem, forasmuch as the taking Mr. Bacon again into the Council was first to keep him out of the Assembly, and in the next place the Governor knew the country people were hastening down with dreadful threatenings to doubly revenge all wrongs should be done to Mr. Bacon or his men, or whoever should have had the least hand in them.

In three or four days after this escape, upon news that Mr. Bacon was thirty miles up the river, at the head of four hundred men, the Governor sent to the parts adjacent, on both sides James River, for the militia and all the men could be got to come and defend the town. Expresses came almost hourly of the army's approaches, who in less than four days after the first account of them, at two of the clock, entered the town, without being withstood, and formed a body upon a green, not a flight shot from the end of the state house, of horse and foot, as well regular as veteran troops, who forthwith possessed themselves of all the avenues, disarming all in town, and coming thither in boats or by land.

In half an hour after this the drum beat for the House to meet, and in less than an hour more Mr. Bacon came with a file of fusiliers on either hand, near the corner of the state house, where the Governor and Council went forth to him. We saw from the window the Governor open his breast, and Bacon strutting betwixt his two files of men, with his left arm on Kenbow, flinging his right arm every way, both like men distracted; and if, in this moment of fury, that enraged multitude had fallen upon the Governor and Council, we of the Assembly expected the same immediate fate. I stepped down, and amongst the crowd of spectators found the seamen of my sloop, who prayed me not to stir from them, when, in two minutes, the Governor walked towards his private apartment, a quoit's cast distant, at the other end of the state house, the gentlemen of the Council following him; and after them walked Mr. Bacon with outrageous postures of his head, arms, body, and legs, often tossing his hand from his sword to his hat, and after him came a detachment of fusiliers (muskets not being there in use), who with their locks bent presented their fusils at a window of the Assembly chamber filled with faces, repeating with menacing voices, "We will have it, we will have it," half a minute, when as one of our House, a person known to many of them, shook his handkerchief out at the window, saying, "You shall have it, you shall have it," three or four times; at these words they set down their fusils, unbent their locks, and stood still until Bacon coming back, they followed him to their main body. In this hubbub a servant of mine got so nigh as to hear the Governor's words, and also followed Mr. Bacon and heard what he said, who came and told me that when the Governor opened his breast, he said: "Here! shoot me. 'Fore God, fair mark! shoot!" often rehearsing the same, without any other words; whereto Mr. Bacon answered: "No, may it please your Honor, we will not hurt a hair of your head, nor of any other man's; we are come for a commission to save our lives from the Indians, which you have so often promised, and now we will have it before we go."

But when Mr. Bacon followed the Governor and Council with the forementioned impetuous (like delirious) actions, whilst that party presented their fusils at the window full of faces, he said: "Damn my blood, I'll kill Governor, Council, Assembly, and all, and then I'll sheathe my sword in my own heart's blood"; and afterwards 'twas said Bacon had given a signal to his men who presented their fusils at those gazing out at the window, that if he should draw his sword they were on sight of it to fire, and slay us; so near was the massacre of us all that very minute, had Bacon in that paroxysm of frantic fury but drawn his sword before the pacific handkerchief was shaken out at window.

In an hour or more after these violent concussions, Mr. Bacon came up to our chamber and desired a commission from us to go against the Indians. Our speaker sat silent, when one Mr. Blayton, a neighbor to Mr. Bacon and elected with him a member of Assembly for the same county (who therefore durst speak to him), made answer: "'Twas not in our province or power, nor of any other, save the King's viceregent, our governor." He pressed hard nigh half an hour's harangue on the preserving our lives from the Indians, inspecting the public revenues, the exorbitant taxes, and redressing the grievances and calamities of that deplorable country, whereto having no other answer, he went away dissatisfied.

Little expecting to hear of more intestine broils, I went home to Potomac, where reports were afterwards various. We had account that General Bacon was marched with a thousand men into the forest to seek the enemy Indians, and in a few days after our next news was that the Governor had summoned together the militia of Gloucester and Middlesex Counties to the number of twelve hundred men, and proposed to them to follow and suppress that rebel Bacon; whereupon arose a murmuring before his face, "Bacon, Bacon, Bacon," and all walked out of the field, muttering as they went, "Bacon, Bacon, Bacon," leaving the Governor and those that came with him to themselves, who being thus abandoned wafted over Chesapeake Bay thirty miles to Accomac.

Mr. Bacon, hearing of this, came back part of the way, and sent out parties of horse patrolling through every county, carrying away prisoners all whom he distrusted might any more molest his Indian persecution, yet giving liberty to such as pledged him their oaths to return home and live quiet; the copies or contents of which oaths I never saw, but heard were very strict, though little observed.

The Governor made a second attempt, coming over from Accomac with what men he could procure in sloops and boats forty miles up the river to Jamestown, which Bacon hearing of, came again down from his forest pursuit, and finding a bank not a flight shot long cast up thwart the neck of the peninsula there in Jamestown, he stormed it, and took the town, in which attack were twelve men slain and wounded, but the Governor with most of his followers fled back down the river in their vessels.

Here, resting a few days, they concerted the burning of the town, wherein Mr. Lawrence and Mr. Drumond, owning the two best houses save one, set fire each to his own house, which example the soldiers following, laid the whole town (with church and state house) in ashes, saying the rogues should harbor no more there.

On these reiterated molestations, Bacon calls a convention at Middle Plantation, fifteen miles from Jamestown, in the month of August, 1676, where an oath with one or more proclamations were formed, and writs by him issued for an Assembly. The oaths or writs I never saw, but one proclamation commanded all men in the land on pain of death to join him, and retire into the wilderness upon arrival of the forces expected from England, and oppose them until they should propose or accept to treat of an accommodation, which we who lived comfortably could not have undergone, so as the whole land must have become an Aceldama if God's exceeding mercy had not timely removed him.

During these tumults in Virginia a second danger menaced Maryland by an insurrection in that province, complaining of their heavy taxes, etc., where two or three of the leading malcontents (men otherwise of laudable characters) were put to death, which stifled the further spreading of that flame. Mr. Bacon (at this time) pressed the best ship in James River, carrying twenty guns, and putting into her his lieutenant general, Mr. Bland, and under him the forementioned Captain Carver, formerly a commander of merchants' ships, with men and all necessaries, he sent her to ride before Accomac to curb and intercept all smaller vessels of war commissioned by the Governor, coming often over and making depredations on the western shore, as if we had been foreign enemies.

Now returning to Captain Carver, the Governor sent for him to come on shore, promising his peaceable return, who answered, "He could not trust his word, but if he would send his hand and seal, he would adventure to wait upon his Honor," which was done, and Carver went in his sloop well armed and manned with the most trusty of his men, where he was caressed with wine, etc., and large promises, if he would forsake Bacon, resign his ship, or join with him; to all which he answered that if he served the devil he would be true to his trust, but that he was resolved to go home and live quiet.

In the time of this reception and parley, an armed boat was prepared with many oars in a creek not far off, but out of sight, which when Carver sailed, rowed out of the creek, and it being almost calm the boat outwent the sloop, whilst all on board the ship were upon the deck, staring at both, thinking the boat's company coming on board by Carver's invitation to be civilly entertained in requital of the kindness they supposed he had received on shore, until coming under the stern, those in the boat slipped nimbly in at the gunroom ports with pistols, etc., when one courageous gentleman ran up to the deck, and clapped a pistol to Bland's breast, saying, "You are my prisoner," the boat's company suddenly following with pistols, swords, etc., and after Captain Larimore (the commander of the ship before she was pressed) having from the highest and hindmost part of the stern interchanged a signal from the shore by flirting his handkerchief about his nose, his own former crew had laid handspikes ready, which they (at that instant) caught up, etc., so as Bland and Carver's men were amazed, and yielded.

Carver, seeing a hurly-burly on the ship's deck, would have gone away with his sloop, but having little wind and the ship threatening to sink him, he tamely came on board, where Bland and he with their party were laid in irons and in three or four days Carver was hanged on shore. . . . Mr. Bacon now returns from his last expedition sick of a flux, without finding any enemy Indians, having not gone far by reason of the vexations behind him; nor had he one dry day in all his marches to and fro in the forest, whilst the plantations (not fifty miles distant) had a summer so dry as stinted the Indian corn and tobacco, etc., which the people ascribed to the powwowings (i.e. the sorceries of the Indians). In a while Bacon dies and was succeeded by his Lieutenant General and so all submitted and were pardoned, exempting those nominated and otherwise proscribed, in a proclamation of indemnity, the principal of whom were Lawrence and Drumond.

Mr. Bland was then a prisoner, having been taken with Carver, as before is noted, and in a few days Mr. Drumond was brought in, when the Governor, being on board a ship, came immediately to shore and complimented him with the ironical sarcasm of a low bend, saying: "Mr. Drumond! you are very welcome; I am more glad to see you than any man in Virginia. Mr. Drumond, you shall be hanged in half an hour"; who answered, "What your Honor pleases"; and as soon as a council of war could meet, his sentence be dispatched and a gibbet erected (which took up near two hours), he was executed.

The last account of Mr. Lawrence was from an uppermost plantation, whence he and four others, desperadoes, with horses, pistols, etc., marched away in a snow ankle-deep, who were thought to have cast themselves into a branch of some river, rather than to be treated like Drumond.

Bacon's body was so made away, as his bones were never found to be exposed on a gibbet as was purposed, stones being laid in his coffin, supposed to be done by Lawrence.

Near this time arrived a small fleet with a regiment from England, Sir John Berry, admiral; Colonel Herbert Jefferyes, commander of the land forces; and Colonel Morrison, who had one year been a former governor. There, all three joined in commission with or to Sir William Barclay, soon after when a general court and also an Assembly were held, where some of our former Assembly (with so many others) were put to death, divers whereof were persons of honest reputations and handsome estates, as that the Assembly petitioned the Governor to spill no more blood; and Mr. Presley, at his coming home, told me he believed the Governor would have hanged half the country if they had let him alone. The first was Mr. Bland, whose friends in England had procured his pardon to be sent over with the fleet, which he pleaded at his trial was in the Governor's pocket, but he was answered by Colonel Morrison that he pleaded his pardon at sword's point, which was looked upon an odd sort of reply, and he was executed; as was talked, by private instructions from England, the Duke of York having sworn, "By God, Bacon and Bland should die."

The Governor went in the fleet to London, leaving Colonel Jefferyes in his place, and by next shipping came back a person who waited on his Honor in his voyage (and until his death), from whom a report was whispered about, that the King did say, "That old fool has hanged more men in that naked country than he had done for the murder of his father"; whereof the Governor hearing died soon after, without having seen his Majesty — which shuts up this tragedy.

The Virginia Rebellion in the Seventeenth Century, by T.M.

# 11. The Men of Maine

*Maine was more difficult to colonize than other parts of coastal New England; its isolated inhabitants early developed traits peculiar to them. The principal promoter of settlement was Sir Ferdinando Gorges, who shared with John Mason a wide grant of land north of Massachusetts, and who soon took everything between the Piscataqua and the Kennebec rivers for his share. But aggressive Puritan emigrants from Massachusetts moved into the territory and became the dominant element. By 1650 the Bay Colony had annexed all the scattered Maine settlements. One of the men most irritated by this expansion of Massachusetts was John Josselyn, whose brother was a principal representative in New England of the aggrieved Gorges and Mason heirs. In writing of his voyages he spoke highly of the sturdy men of Maine, and with sly hostility of their neighbors; it is clear that the Maine men he did not like were those who had come up from the south.*

THE PEOPLE in the province of Maine may be divided into magistrates, husbandmen or planters, and fishermen; of the magistrates some be royalists, the rest perverse spirits, the like are the planters and fishers, of which some be planters and fishers both, others mere fishers.

Handicraftsmen there are but few, the cooper, smiths and carpenters are best welcome amongst them, shopkeepers there are none, being supplied by the Massachusetts merchant with all things they stand in need of, keeping here and there fair magazines stored with English goods, but they set excessive prices on them; if they do not gain cent per cent, they cry out that they are losers. Hence English shoes are sold for eight and nine shillings a pair; worsted stockings of three shillings sixpence a pair for seven and eight shillings a pair; dowlas that is sold in England for one- or two-and-twenty pence an ell, for four shillings a yard; serges of two shillings or three shillings a yard, for six and seven shillings a yard; and so all sorts of commodities both for planters and fishermen.

The planters are or should be restless painstakers, providing for their cattle, planting and sowing of corn, fencing their grounds, cutting and bringing home fuel, cleaving of clawboard [clapboard] and pipe staves; fishing for fresh-water fish and fowling takes up most of their time, if not all; the diligent hand maketh rich, but if they be of a dronish disposition, as some are, they become wretchedly poor and miserable, scarce able to free themselves and family from importunate famine, especially in the winter for want of bread.

They have a custom of taking tobacco, sleeping at noon, sitting long at meals, sometimes four times in a day, and now and then drinking a dram of the bottle extraordinarily: the smoking of tobacco, if moderately used, refresheth the weary much, and so doth sleep.

> A traveler five hours doth crave
> To sleep, a student seven will have,
> And nine sleeps every idle knave.

The physician allows but three draughts at a meal, the first for need, the second for pleasure, and the third for sleep; but little observed by them, unless they have no other liquor to drink but water. In some places where the springs are frozen up, or at least the way to their springs made unpassable by reason of the snow and the like, they dress their meat in aqua caelestis, i.e. melted snow. At other times it is very well cooked, and they feed upon (generally) as good flesh, beef, pork, mutton, fowl, and fish as any is in the whole world besides.

Their servants, which are for the most part English, when they are out of their time, will not work under half a crown a day, although it be for to make hay, and for less I do not see how they can, by reason of the dearness of clothing. If they hire them by the year, they pay them fourteen or fifteen pound, yea, twenty pound at the year's end in corn, cattle, and fish; some of these prove excellent fowlers, bringing in as many as will maintain their master's house, besides the profit that accrues by their feathers. They use (when it is to be had) a great round shot, called Barstable shot (which is best for fowl), made of a lead blacker than our common lead; to six pound of shot they allow one pound of powder; cannon powder is esteemed best.

The fishermen take yearly upon the coasts many hundred kentles of cod, hake, haddock, pollack, etc., which they split, salt, and dry at their stages, making three voyages in a year. When they share their fish (which is at the end of every voyage) they separate the best from the worst; the first they call merchantable fish, being sound, full-grown fish and well made up, which is known when it is clear like a lanthorn horn and without spots; the second sort they call refuse fish — that is, such as is salt-burnt, spotted, rotten, and carelessly ordered: these they put off to the Massachusetts merchants; the merchantable for thirty and two-and-thirty ryals a kentle [a hundred-and-twelve-pound weight]; the refuse for nine shillings and ten shillings a kentle.

The merchant sends the merchantable fish to Lisbon, Bilbao, Bordeaux, Marseilles, Toulon, Rochelle, Rouen, and other cities of France, to the Canaries with clawboard and pipe staves, which is there and at the Caribs a prime commodity; the refuse fish they put off at the Carib Islands, Barbados, Jamaica, etc., who feed their Negroes with it.

To every shallop belong four fishermen — a master or steersman, a midshipman, and a foremastman — and a shore man who washes it out of the salt, and dries it upon hurdles pitched upon stakes breast-high and tends their cookery; these often get in one voyage eight or nine pound a man for their shares, but it doth some of them little good for the merchant to increase his gains by putting off his commodity in the midst of their voyages, and at the end thereof comes in with a walking tavern, a bark laden with the legitimate blood of the rich grape, which they bring from Fayal, Madeira, Canaries, with brandy, rum, the Barbados strong water, and tobacco. Coming ashore he gives them a taster or two, which so charms them that for no persuasions that their employers can use will they go out to sea, although fair and seasonable weather, for two or three days — nay, sometimes a whole week — till they are wearied with drinking, taking ashore two or three hogsheads of wine and rum to drink off when the merchant is gone. If a man of quality chance to come where they are roistering and gulling in wine with a dear felicity, he must be sociable and rollypooly [rolypoly, i.e., he must play the game] with them, taking of their liberal cups as freely, or else be gone, which is best for him. When the day of payment comes, they may justly complain of their costly sin of drunkenness, for their shares will do no more than pay the reckoning; if they save a kentle or two to buy shoes and stockings, shirts, and waistcoats with, 'tis well; otherwise they must enter into the merchant's books for such things as they stand in need of, becoming thereby the merchant's slaves, and when it riseth to a big sum are constrained to mortgage their plantation if they have any; the merchant when the time is expired is sure to seize upon their plantation and stock of cattle, turning them out of house and home, poor creatures, to look out for a new habitation in some remote place, where they begin the world again. The lavish planters have the same fate, partaking with them in the like bad husbandry.

JOHN JOSSELYN, An Account of Two Voyages to New England

# 12. William Byrd Discovers Lubberland

*If sophisticated observers could deride the simple, hardy, and not altogether puritanical people of Maine, much more could they make fun of the lazy and ignorant inhabitants of the backwoods of North Carolina. Some coastal settlements of that province, notably Edenton, could vie with any in the country in elegance. But the back country was filled — so Virginians and South Carolinians alleged — by an uncouth, indolent, and loutish race. William Byrd II of "Westover" had some reason for looking down on such folk. Educated in England, a member of the Royal Society, the possessor at his estate on the James of one of the largest libraries in America, he was a man of taste, whose Writings contain some very amusing and instructive matter. His travels in North Carolina excited his satirical inclinations, and much of what he says is highly unfair. But it was at least authentic humor. The North Carolinians, he wrote, "keep so many sabbaths every week that their disregard of the seventh day has no manner of cruelty in it either to servants or cattle."*

SURELY there is no place in the world where the inhabitants live with less labor than in North Carolina. It approaches nearer to the description of Lubberland than any other, by the great felicity of the climate, the easiness of raising provisions, and the slothfulness of the people. Indian corn is of so great increase that a little pains will subsist a very large family with bread, and then they may have meat without any pains at all, by the help of the low grounds, and the great variety of mast that grows on the highland. The men, for their parts, just like the Indians, impose all the work on the poor women. They make their wives rise out of their beds early in the morning, at the same time that they lie and snore, till the sun has risen one-third of his course and dispersed all the unwholesome damps. Then, after stretching and yawning for half an hour, they light their pipes, and, under the protection of a cloud of smoke, venture out into the open air; though, if it happens to be never so little cold, they quickly return shivering into the chimney corner. When the weather is mild, they stand leaning with both their arms upon the cornfield fence, and gravely consider whether they had best go and take a small heat at the hoe, but generally find reasons to put it off till another time. Thus they loiter away their lives, like Solomon's sluggard, with their arms across, and at the winding up of the year scarcely have bread to eat. To speak the truth, it is a thorough aversion to labor that makes people file off to North Carolina, where plenty and a warm sun confirm them in their disposition to laziness for their whole lives.

Provisions here are extremely cheap and extremely good, so that people may live plentifully at a trifling expense. Nothing is dear but law, physic, and strong drink, which are all bad in their kind, and the last they get with so much difficulty, that they are never guilty of the sin of suffering it to sour upon their hands. Their vanity generally lies not so much in having a handsome dining room, as a handsome house or office; in this kind of structure they are really extravagant. They are rarely guilty of flattering or making any court to their governors, but treat them with all the excesses of freedom and familiarity. They are of opinion their rulers would be apt to grow insolent, if they grew rich, and for that reason take care to keep them poorer, and more dependent, if possible, than the saints in New England used to do their governors. They have very little corn, so they are forced to carry on their home traffic with paper money. This is the only cash that will tarry in the country, and for that reason the discount goes on increasing between that and real money, and will do so to the end of the chapter.

WILLIAM BYRD, A Journey to the Land of Eden

# 13. Sarah Knight Travels from Boston to New York

*Just as amusing as William Byrd's work, equally satirical, and even more vivid is the record which Sarah Kemble Knight, a Boston schoolmistress and woman of affairs, wrote of her journey to New York at a period when such a trip was a serious venture for an unaccompanied woman. She was nearly forty at the time, and clearly a person of vigor. Underneath her sharp condemnation of the abuses and shortcomings from which she suffered is evident a vein of good humor and tolerance. We are not astonished to learn that after she settled at New London, Connecticut, she was indicted and fined for selling liquor to the Indians. Her diary was not written for fame, but for her own amusement, and did not see print until more than a century after her eventful journey.*

MONDAY, October the 2d, 1704. — About three o'clock afternoon, I began my journey from Boston to New Haven; being about two hundred mile. My kinsman, Captain Robert Luist, waited on me as far as Dedham, where I was to meet the western post.

I visited the Reverend M. Belcher, the minister of the town, and tarried there till evening, in hopes the post would come along. But he not coming, I resolved to go to Billings' where he used to lodge, being twelve miles farther. But being ignorant of the way, Madam Belcher, seeing no persuasions of her good spouse's or hers could prevail with me to lodge there that night, very kindly went with me to the tavern, where I hoped to get my guide, and desired the hostess to inquire of her guests whether any of them would go with me. I told her no, I would not be accessory to such extortion.

"Then John shan't go," says she; "no, indeed, shan't he"; and held forth at that rate a long time, that I began to fear I was got among the quaking tribe, believing not a limber-tongued sister among them could outdo Madam Hostess.

Upon this, to my no small surprise, son John arose, and gravely demanded what I would give him to go with me. "Give you?" says I. "Are you John?" "Yes," says he, "for want of a better"; and behold! this John looked as old as my host, and perhaps had been a man in the last century. "Well, Mr. John," says I, "make your demands." "Why, half a piece of eight and a dram," says John. I agreed, and gave him a dram (now) in hand to bind the bargain.

My hostess catechized John for going so cheap, saying his poor wife would break her heart. . . .

When we had ridden about an hour, we came into a thick swamp, which by reason of a great fog, very much startled me, it being now very dark. But nothing dismayed John: he had encountered a thousand and a thousand such swamps, having a universal knowledge in the woods; and readily answered all my inquiries, which were not a few.

In about an hour, or something more, after we left the swamp, we came to Billings', where I was to lodge. My guide dismounted and very complacently helped me down and showed the door, signing to me with his hand to go in; which I gladly did—but had not gone many steps into the room, ere I was interrogated by a young lady I understood afterwards was the eldest daughter of the family, with these, or words to this purpose; viz., "Law for me!—what in the world brings you here at this time of night? I never see a woman on the road so dreadful late in all the days of my versal life. Who are you? Where are you going? I'm scared out of my wits!" — with much more of the same kind. I stood aghast, preparing to reply, when in comes my guide — to him Madam turned, roaring out: "Lawful heart, John, is it you? — how de do! Where in the world are you going with this woman? Who is she?" John made no answer, but sat down in the corner, fumbled out his black junk, and saluted that instead of Deb; she then turned again to me and fell anew into her silly questions, without asking me to sit down.

I told her she treated me very rudely, and I did not think it my duty to answer her unmannerly questions. But to get rid of them, I told her I came there to have the post's company with me tomorrow on my journey, etc. Miss stared awhile, drew a chair, bade me sit, and then ran up stairs and put on two or three rings (or else I had not seen them before), and returning, set herself just before me, showing the way to Reading, that I might see her ornaments, perhaps to gain the more respect. But her granam's new rung sow, had it appeared, would have affected me as much. I paid honest John with money and dram according to contract, and dismissed him, and prayed Miss to show me where I must lodge. She conducted me to a parlor in a little back lean-to, which was almost filled with the bedstead, which was so high that I was forced to climb on a chair to get up to the wretched bed that lay on it; on which having stretched my tired limbs, and laid my head on a sad-colored pillow, I began to think on the transactions of the past day.

Tuesday, October the 3d, about eight in the morning, I with the post proceeded forward without observing anything remarkable; and about two, afternoon, arrived at the post's second stage, where the western post met him and exchanged letters. Here, having called for something to eat, the woman brought in a twisted thing like a cable, but something whiter; and, laying in on the board, tugged for life to bring it into a capacity to spread; which having with great pains accomplished, she served in a dish of pork and cabbage, I suppose the remains of dinner. The sauce was of deep purple, which I thought was boiled in her dye kettle; the bread was Indian, and everything on the table service agreeable to these. I, being hungry, got a little down; but my stomach was soon cloyed, and what cabbage I swallowed served me for a cud the whole day after.

Having here discharged the ordinary for self and guide (as I understood was the custom), about three afternoon went on with my third guide. . . .

Being come to Mr. Haven's, I was very civilly received and courteously entertained, in a clean, comfortable house; and the good woman was very active in helping off my riding clothes, and then asked what I would eat. I told her I had some chocolate, if she would prepare it; which with the help of some milk, and a little clean brass kettle, she soon effected to my satisfaction. I then betook me to my apartment, which was a little room parted from the kitchen by a single board partition; where, after I had noted the occurrences of the past day, I went to bed, which, though pretty hard, yet neat and handsome. But I could get no sleep, because of the clamor of some of the town topers in next room, who were entered into a strong debate concerning the signification of the name of their country, viz. Narragansett. One said it was named so by the Indians, because there grew a brier there, of a prodigious height and bigness, the like hardly ever known, called by the Indians narragansett; and quotes an Indian of so barbarous a name for his author, that I could not write it. His antagonist replied no — it was from a spring it had its name, which he well knew where it was, which was extreme cold in summer, and as hot as could be imagined in the winter, which was much resorted to by the natives, and by them called narragansett (hot and cold), and that was the original notice, which he uttered with such a roaring voice and thundering of their place's name — with a thousand impertinences not worth blows with the fist of wickedness on the table, that it pierced my very head. I heartily fretted, and wished them tongue-tied; but with as little success as a friend of mine once, who was (as she said) kept a whole night awake, on a journey, by a country lieutenant and a sergeant, ensign, and a deacon, contriving how to bring a triangle into a square. They kept calling for t'other gill, which, while they were swallowing, was some intermission; but, presently, like oil to fire, increased the flame. I set my candle on a chest by the bedside, and sitting up, fell to my old way of composing my resentments, in the following manner:

I ask thy aid, O potent Rum!
To charm these wrangling topers dumb.
Thou hast their giddy brains possest —

> The man confounded with the beast —
> And I, poor I, can get no rest.
> Intoxicate them with thy fumes:
> O still their tongues till morning comes!

And I know not but my wishes took effect; for the dispute soon ended with t'other dram; and so good night!

Wednesday, October 4th. — About four in the morning we set out for Kingston with a French doctor in our company. He and the post put on very furiously, so that I could not keep up with them, only as now and then they would stop till they saw me. This road was poorly furnished with accommodations for travelers, so that we were forced to ride twenty-two miles by the post's account, but nearer thirty by mine, before we could bait [feed] so much as our horses, which I exceedingly complained of. But the post encouraged me, by saying we should be well accommodated anon at Mr. Devil's, a few miles farther. But I questioned whether we ought to go to the devil to be helped out of affliction. However, like the rest of deluded souls that post to the infernal den, we made all possible speed to this devil's habitation; where alighting, in full assurance of good accommodation, we were going in. But meeting his two daughters, as I supposed twins — they so nearly resembled each other, both in features and habit, and looked as old as the devil himself, and quite as ugly — we desired entertainment, but could hardly get a word out of them, till with our importunity, telling them our necessity, etc., they called the old sophister, who was as sparing of his words as his daughters had been, and no, or none, were the replies he made us to our demands. He differed only in this from the old fellow in t'other country: he let us depart.

Thus leaving this habitation of cruelty, we went forward; and arriving at an ordinary about two miles farther, found tolerable accommodation. But our hostess, being a pretty full-mouthed old creature, entertained our fellow traveler, the French doctor, with innumerable complaints of her bodily infirmities; and whispered to him so loud that all the house had as full a hearing as he: which was very diverting to the company (of which there was a great many), as one might see by their sneering. But poor weary I slipped out to enter my mind in my journal, and left my great landlady with her talkative guests to themselves.

Thursday, October the 5th, about three in the afternoon, I set forward with neighbor Polly and Jemima, a girl about eighteen years old, who he said he had been to fetch out of the Narragansetts, and said they had rode thirty miles that day, on a sorry lean jade, with only a bag under her for a pillion, which the poor girl often complained was very uneasy.

About seven that evening we came to New London ferry; here, by reason of a very high wind, we met with great difficulty in getting over — the boat tossed exceedingly, and our horses capered at a very surprising rate, and set us all in a fright, especially poor Jemima, who desired her father to say "So, Jack" to the jade, to make her stand. But the careless parent taking no notice of her repeated desires, she roared out in a passionate manner: "Pray sooth, father; are you deaf? Say 'So, Jack' to the jade, I tell you." The dutiful parent obeys, saying "So, Jack; so, Jack," as gravely as if he'd been to saying catechize after young Miss, who with her fright looked of all colors in the rainbow.

Being safely arrived at the house of Mrs. Prentice's in New London, I treated neighbor Polly and daughter for their diverting company, and bade them farewell; and between nine and ten at night waited on the Reverend Mr. Gurdon Saltonstall, minister of the town, who kindly invited me to stay that night at his house, where I was very handsomely and plentifully treated and lodged; and made good the great character I had before heard concerning him, viz., that he was the most affable, courteous, generous, and best of men.

Friday, October 6th. — I got up very early, in order to hire somebody to go with me to New Haven, being in great perplexity at the thoughts of proceeding alone; which my most hospitable entertainer observing, himself went and soon returned with a young gentleman of the town, whom he could confide in to go with me. . . . The roads all along this way are very bad, encumbered with rocks and mountainous passages, which were very disagreeable to my tired carcass; but we went on with a moderate pace which made the journey more pleasant. But after about eight miles riding, in going over a bridge under which the river ran very swift, my horse stumbled and very narrowly 'scaped falling over into the water, which extremely frightened me. But through God's goodness I met with no harm, and mounting again, in about half a mile's riding, came to an ordinary, was well entertained by a woman of about seventy and vantage, but of as sound intellectuals as one of seventeen.

Saturday, October 7th. — About two o'clock afternoon we arrived at New Haven, where I was received with all possible prospects and civility. Here I discharged Mr. Wheeler with a reward to his satisfaction, and took some time to rest after so long and toilsome a journey; and informed myself of the manners and customs of the place, and at the same time employed myself in the affair I went there upon.

They are governed by the same laws as we in Boston (or little differing), throughout this whole colony of Connecticut, and much the same way of church government, and many of them good, sociable people, and I hope religious too: but a little too much independent in their principles, and, as I have been told, were formerly in their zeal very rigid in their administrations towards such as their laws made offenders, even to a harmless kiss or innocent merriment among young people, whipping being a frequent and counted an easy punishment, about which as other crimes, the judges were absolute in their sentences.

Their diversions in this part of the country are on lecture days and training days mostly; on the former there is riding from town to town. And on training days the youth divert themselves by shooting at the target, as they call it (but it very much resembles a pillory), where he that hits nearest the white has some yards of red ribbon presented him, which being tied to his hatband, the two ends streaming down his back, he is led away in triumph, with great applause, as the winners of the Olympic games. They generally marry very young: the males oftener, as I am told, under twenty than above: they generally make public weddings, and have a way something singular (as they say) in some of them, viz., just before joining hands the bridegroom quits the place, who is soon followed by the bridesmen, and as it were dragged back to duty — being the reverse to the former practice among us, to steal mistress bride. And they generally lived very well and comfortably in their families. But too indulgent (especially the farmers) to their slaves: suffering too great familiarity from them, permitting them to sit at the table and eat with them (as they say to save time), and into the dish goes the black hoof as freely as the white hand. They told me that there was a farmer lived near the town where I lodged who had some difference with his slave, concerning something the master had promised him and did not punctually perform, which caused some hard words between them; but at length they put the matter to arbitration and bound themselves to stand to the ward of such as they named — which done, the arbitrators, having heard the allegations of both parties, ordered the master to pay forty shillings to blackface and acknowledge his fault. And so the matter ended, the poor master very honestly standing to the award. . . .

Being at a merchant's house, in comes a tall country fellow, with his alfogeos [cheeks] full of tobacco; for they seldom loose their cud, but keep chewing and spitting as long as their eyes are open — he advanced to the middle of the room, makes an awkward nod, and spitting a large deal of aromatic tincture, he gave a scrape with his shovel-like shoe, leaving a small shovelful of dirt on the floor, made a full stop, hugging his own pretty body with his hands under his arms, stood staring round him, like a cat let out of a basket. At last, like the creature Balaam rode on, he opened his mouth and said, "Have you any ribinen for hatbands to sell, I pray?" The questions and answers about the pay being past, the ribbon is brought and opened. Bumpkin Simpers cries, "It's confounded gay, I vow"; and beckoning to the door, in comes Joan Tawdry, dropping about fifty curtsies, and stands by him; he shows her the ribbon. "Law, you," says she, "it's right gent, do you take it, 'tis dreadful pretty." Then she inquires, "Have you any hood silk, I pray?" which being brought and bought, "Have you any thread silk to sew it with?" says she; which being accommodated with, they departed. They generally stand after they come in a great while speechless, and sometimes don't say a word till they are asked what they want, which I impute to the awe they stand in of the merchants, who they are constantly almost indebted to, and must take what they bring without liberty to choose for themselves; but they serve them as well, making the merchants stay long enough for their pay.

December 6th. — Being by this time well recruited and rested after my journey, my business lying unfinished by some concerns at New York depending thereupon, my kinsman, Mr. Thomas

Trowbridge, of New Haven, must needs take a journey there before it could be accomplished; I resolved to go there in company with him and a man of the town which I engaged to wait on me there. Accordingly, December 6th, we set out from New Haven, and about eleven same morning came to Stratford ferry; which crossing, about two miles on the other side baited our horses and would have eat a morsel ourselves, but the pumpkin and Indian mixed bread had such an aspect, and the barelegged punch so awkward or rather awful a sound, that we left both, and proceeded forward, and about seven at night came to Fairfield, where we met with good entertainment and lodged; and early next morning set forward to Norrowalk, from its half-Indian name "North-walk", where about twelve at noon we arrived, and had a dinner of fried venison, very savory. Landlady, wanting some pepper in the seasoning, bid the girl hand her the spice in the little "gay" cup on the shelf. From hence we hastened towards Rye, walking and leading our horses near a mile together, up a prodigious high hill; and so riding till about nine at night, and there arrived and took up our lodgings at an ordinary, which a French family kept. Here being very hungry, I desired a fricassee, which the Frenchman, undertaking, managed so contrary to my notion of cookery, that I hastened to bed supperless; and being shown the way up a pair of stairs which had such a narrow passage that I had almost stopped by the bulk of my body, but arriving at my apartment found it to be a little lean-to chamber, furnished among other rubbish with a high bed and a low one, a long table, a bench, and a bottomless chair. Little Miss went to scratch up my kennel, which rustled as if she had been in the barn among the husks, and suppose such was the contents of the ticking. Nevertheless, being exceeding weary, down I laid my poor carcass (never more tired), and found my covering as scanty as my bed was hard. Anon I heard another rustling noise in the room — called to know the matter — little Miss said she was making a bed for the men; who, when they were in bed, complained their legs lay out of it by reason of its shortness. My poor bones complained bitterly, not being used to such lodgings, and so did the man who was with us; and poor I made but one groan, which was from the time I went to bed to the time I rose, which was about three in the morning, sitting up by the fire till light, and, having discharged our ordinary — which was as dear as if we had had far better fare — we took our leave of Monsieur and about seven in the morning came to New Rochelle, a French town, where we had a good breakfast. And on the strength of that about an hour before sunset got to York.

The Journals of Madam Knight

# 14. German Redemptioners Take Ship to Pennsylvania

*The problem of refugees is as old as the fact of man's inhumanity to man. Early in the eighteenth century many thousands of Germans from the Palatinate and other parts of the Rhineland took shelter in England, with grave embarrassment to the authorities. In 1710 three thousand were sent on to New York under the care of Robert Hunter, governor of that province. Some went to the Mohawk Valley; some reached the Susquehanna and other parts of Pennsylvania. Swiss Mennonites meanwhile came into the district about Lancaster, Pennsylvania. The hospitable province of the Penns was especially congenial to emigrants, and the main stream of German settlers poured into it; for thirty years beginning in 1727 an average of about two thousand a year came over. They made thrifty, enterprising farmers and loyal subjects of the king. Many were so poor that they could not pay their passage. They therefore became "redemptioners," selling their services for a term of years to obtain transportation and initial support. Any voyage in those days, as Dr. Johnson recognized when he compared ships with prisons, was a misery, but the poverty-stricken immigrants got especially rough treatment.*

WHEN the ships have for the last time weighed their anchors near the city of Kaupp [Cowes] in Old England, the real misery begins with the long voyage. For from there the ships, unless they have good wind, must often sail eight, nine, ten to twelve weeks before they reach Philadelphia. But even with the best wind the voyage lasts seven weeks.

But during the voyage there is on board these ships terrible misery, stench, fumes, horror, vomiting, many kinds of seasickness, fever, dysentery, headache, heat, constipation, boils, scurvy, cancer, mouth rot, and the like, all of which come from old and sharply-salted food and meat, also from very bad and foul water, so that many die miserably.

Add to this want of provisions, hunger, thirst, frost, heat, damp-ness, anxiety, want, afflictions and lamentations, together with other trouble, as *e.g.,* the lice abound so frightfully, especially on sick people, that they can be scraped off the body. The misery reaches a climax when a gale rages for two or three nights and days, so that every one believes that the ship will go to the bottom with all human beings on board. In such a visitation the people cry and pray most piteously.

Among the healthy, impatience sometimes grows so great and cruel that one curses the other, or himself and the day of his birth, and sometimes come near killing each other. Misery and malice join each other, so that they cheat and rob one another. One always reproaches the other with having persuaded him to undertake the journey. Frequently children cry out against their parents, hus-bands against their wives, and wives against their husbands; brothers and sisters, friends and acquaintances, against each other. But most against the soul-traffickers.

No one can have an idea of the sufferings which women in con-finement have to bear with their innocent children on board these ships. Few of this class escape with their lives; many a mother is cast into the water with her child as soon as she is dead. One day, just as we had a heavy gale, a woman in our ship, who was to give birth and could not give birth under the circumstances, was pushed through a loophole [porthole] in the ship and dropped into the sea, because she was far in the rear of the ship and could not be brought forward.

Children from one to seven years rarely survive the voyage; and many a time parents are compelled to see their children mis-erably suffer and die from hunger, thirst, and sickness, and then to see them cast into the water. I witnessed such misery in no less than thirty-two children in our ship, all of whom were thrown into the sea. The parents grieve all the more since their children find no resting place in the earth, but are devoured by the monsters of the sea. It is a notable fact that children who have not yet had the measles or smallpox generally get them on board the ship, and mostly die of them.

When the ships have landed at Philadelphia after their long voyage, no one is permitted to leave them except those who pay for their passage or can give good security; the others, who cannot pay, must remain on board the ships till they are purchased and are released from the ships by their purchasers. The sick always fare the worst, for the healthy are naturally preferred and purchased first; and so the sick and wretched must often remain on board in front of the city for two or three weeks, and frequently die, whereas many a one, if he could pay his debt and were permitted to leave the ship immediately, might recover and remain alive.

The sale of human beings in the market on board the ship is carried on thus: Every day Englishmen, Dutchmen, and High German people come from the city of Philadelphia and other places, in part from a great distance, say twenty, thirty, or forty hours away, and go on board the newly-arrived ship that has brought and offers for sale passengers from Europe, and select among the healthy persons such as they deem suitable for their business, and bargain with them how long they will serve for their passage money, which most of them are still in debt for. When they have come to an agreement, it happens that adult persons bind themselves in writing to serve three, four, five, or six years for the amount due by them, according to their age and strength. But very young people, from ten to fifteen years, must serve till they are twenty-one years old.

Many parents must sell and trade away their children like so many head of cattle, for if their children take the debt upon themselves, the parents can leave the ship free and unrestrained; but as the parents often do not know where and to what people their children are going, it often happens that such parents and children, after leaving the ship, do not see each other again for many years, perhaps no more in all their lives.

It often happens that whole families, husband, wife, and children, are separated by being sold to different purchasers, especially when they have not paid any part of their passage money.

When a husband or wife has died at sea, when the ship has made more than half of her trip, the survivor must pay or serve not only for himself or herself, but also for the deceased. When both parents have died over halfway at sea, their children, especially when they are young and have nothing to pawn or to pay, must stand for their own and their parents' passage, and serve till they are twenty-one years old. When one has served his or her term, he or she is entitled to a new suit of clothes at parting; and if it has been so stipulated, a man gets in addition a horse, a woman, a cow.

Work and labor in this new and wild land are very hard and manifold, and many a one who came there in his old age must work very hard to his end for his bread. I will not speak of young people. Work mostly consists in cutting wood, felling oak trees, rooting out, or as they say there, clearing large tracts of forest. Such forests, being cleared, are then laid out for fields and meadows. From the best hewn wood, fences are made around the new fields; for there all meadows, orchards, and fruit fields are surrounded and fenced in with planks made of thickly-split wood, laid one above the other, as in zigzag lines, and within such inclosures horses, cattle, and sheep are permitted to graze. Our Europeans who are purchased must always work hard, for new fields are constantly laid out; and so they learn that stumps of oak trees are in America certainly as hard as in Germany.

Gottlieb Mittelberger's Journey to Pennsylvania in the Year 1750

# 15. Benjamin Franklin Arrives in Philadelphia

*It was a memorable day for Pennsylvania and all America when in October, 1723, a seventeen-year-old printer named Benjamin Franklin, who had just quarreled with his half-brother in Boston and left his employ, arrived in Philadelphia.*

*Within seven years he was married, sole owner of a flourishing busi-*
*ness, and publisher of the* Pennsylvania Gazette; *within twenty years*
*he was one of the leaders of the province. Even at seventeen he had*
*schooled himself thoroughly in Addison's writings, and the clear,*
*flowing Addisonian style, as this selection shows, remained one of his*
*important possessions.*

I HAVE been the more particular in this description of my journey, and shall be so of my first entry into that city, that you
may in your mind compare such unlikely beginnings with the
figure I have since made there. I was in my working dress, my
best clothes being to come round by sea. I was dirty from my journey; my pockets were stuffed out with shirts and stockings, and I
knew no soul nor where to look for lodging. I was fatigued with
traveling, rowing, and want of rest; I was very hungry; and my
whole stock of cash consisted of a Dutch dollar and about a shilling
in copper. The latter I gave the people of the boat for my passage,
who at first refused it, on account of my rowing; but I insisted on
their taking it. A man being sometimes more generous when he has
but a little money than when he has plenty, perhaps through fear
of being thought to have but little.

Then I walked up the street, gazing about till near the market
house I met a boy with bread. I had made many a meal on bread,
and, inquiring where he got it, I went immediately to the baker's
he directed me to, in Second Street, and asked for biscuit, intending
such as we had in Boston; but they, it seems, were not made in
Philadelphia. Then I asked for a threepenny loaf, and was told they
had none such. So not considering or knowing the difference of
money, and the greater cheapness nor the names of his bread, I bad
him give me threepennyworth of any sort. He gave me, accordingly,
three great puffy rolls. I was surprised at the quantity, but took it,
and having no room in my pockets, walked off with a roll under
each arm, and eating the other. Thus I went up Market Street as
far as Fourth Street, passing by the door of Mr. Read, my future
wife's father; when she, standing at the door, saw me, and thought
I made, as I certainly did, a most awkward, ridiculous appearance.

Then I turned and went down Chestnut Street and part of Walnut Street, eating my roll all the way, and, coming round, found myself again at Market Street wharf, near the boat I came in, to which I went for a draught of the river water; and, being filled with one of my rolls, gave the other two to a woman and her child that came down the river in the boat with us, and were waiting to go farther.

Thus refreshed, I walked again up the street, which by this time had many clean-dressed people in it, who were all walking the same way. I joined them, and thereby was led into the great meeting house of the Quakers near the market. I sat down among them, and, after looking round awhile and hearing nothing said, being very drowsy through labor and want of rest the preceding night, I fell fast asleep, and continued so till the meeting broke up, when one was kind enough to rouse me. This was, therefore, the first house I was in, or slept in, in Philadelphia.

The Autobiography of Benjamin Franklin

# 16. George Mason Lives in State at Gunston Hall

*Great-grandson of a Cavalier who emigrated to Virginia after Cromwell's men won the battle of Worcester, George Mason inherited some five thousand acres on the Potomac below Alexandria, thus becoming a close neighbor of George Washington. Few Americans of the time had as good an education as his, for his mother hired private tutors and he immersed himself in a library of some fifteen hundred volumes. Although he devoted himself to supervising his estates, declining to employ a manager, he was thoroughly trained in law and government, and Virginia found his services as constitutionalist and legislator invaluable. At the age of thirty, in 1755, he began building one of the famous mansions of tidewater Virginia, Gunston Hall, its architect a skilled craftsman from Oxford. Here he lived the life of gentleman, statesman. and practical planter.*

GUNSTON HALL is situated on a height on the right bank of the Potomac River within a short walk of the shores, and commanding a full view of it, about five miles above the mouth of that branch of it on the same side called the Occoquan. When I can first remember it, it was in a state of high improvement and carefully kept. The south front looked to the river; from an elevated little portico on this front you descended directly into an extensive garden, touching the house on one side and reduced from the natural irregularity of the hilltop to a perfect level platform, the southern extremity of which was bounded by a spacious walk running eastwardly and westwardly, from which there was by the natural and sudden declivity of the hill a rapid descent to the plain considerably below it. On this plain adjoining the margin of the hill, opposite to and in full view from the garden, was a deer park, studded with trees, kept well fenced and stocked with native deer domesticated. On the north front, by which was the principal approach, was an extensive lawn kept closely pastured, through the midst of which led a spacious avenue, girded by long double ranges of that hardy and stately cherry tree, the common blackheart, raised from the stone, and so the more fair and uniform in their growth, commencing at about two hundred feet from the house and extending thence for about twelve hundred feet; the carriageway being in the center and the footways on either side, between the two rows forming each double range of trees, and under their shade.

To the west of the main building were first the schoolhouse, and then at a little distance, masked by a row of large English walnut trees, were the stables. To the east was a high paled yard, adjoining the house, into which opened an outer door from the private front, within or connected with which yard were the kitchen, well, poultry houses, and other domestic arrangements; and beyond it on the same side were the corn house and granary, servants' houses (in those days called Negro quarters), hay yard and cattle pens, all of which were masked by rows of large cherry and mulberry trees. And adjoining the inclosed grounds on which stood the mansion and all these appendages on the eastern side was an extensive pasture for stock of all kinds running down to the river, through which led the road to the Landing, emphatically so called, where all persons or things water-borne were landed or taken off, and where were kept the boats, pettiaugers [piraguas], and canoes, of which there were always several, for business transportation, fishing, and hunting, belonging to the establishment. Farther north and on the same side was an extensive orchard of fine fruit trees of a variety of kinds. Beyond this was a small and highly-fenced pasture devoted to a single brood horse. The occupant in my early days was named Vulcan, of the best stock in the country, and a direct descendant of the celebrated Old James. The west side of the lawn or inclosed grounds was skirted by a wood, just far enough within which to be out of sight was a little village called Log Town, so called because most of the houses were built of hewn pine logs. Here lived several families of the slaves serving about the mansion house; among them were my father's body servant James, a mulatto man and his family, and those of several Negro carpenters.

The heights on which the mansion house stood extended in an east-and-west direction across an isthmus and were at the northern extremity of the estate to which it belonged. This contained something more than five thousand acres and was called Dogue's Neck, water-locked by the Potomac on the south, the Occoquan on the west, and Pohick Creek on the east. The isthmus on the northern boundary is narrow and the whole estate was kept completely inclosed by a fence on that side of about one mile in length, running from the head of Holt's to the margin of Pohick Creek. This fence was maintained with great care and in good repair in my father's time, in order to secure to his own stock the exclusive range within it, and made of uncommon height to keep in the native deer which had been preserved there in abundance from the first settlement of the country and indeed are yet there in considerable numbers. The land south of the heights and comprising more than nine-tenths of the estate was an uniform level elevated some twenty feet above the surface of the river, with the exception of one extensive marsh and three or four water courses, which were accompanied by some ravines and undulations of minor character — and about two-thirds of it were yet clothed with the primitive wood; the whole of this level tract was embraced in one view from the mansion house. In different parts of this tract and detached from each other, my father worked four plantations with his own slaves, each under an overseer, and containing four or five hundred acres of open land. The crops were principally Indian corn and tobacco, the corn for the support of the plantations and the home house, and the tobacco for sale. There was but little small grain made in that part of the country in those days. He had also another plantation worked in the same manner, on an estate he had in Charles County, Maryland, on the Potomac about twenty miles lower down, at a place called Stump Neck.

It was very much the practice with gentlemen of landed and slave estates in the interior of Virginia, so to organize them as to have considerable resources within themselves; to employ and pay but few tradesmen, and to buy little or none of the coarse stuffs and materials used by them; and this practice became stronger and more general during the long period of the Revolutionary War, which in great measure cut off the means of supply from elsewhere. Thus my father had among his slaves carpenters, coopers, sawyers, blacksmiths, tanners, curriers, shoemakers, spinners, weavers and knitters, and even a distiller. His woods furnished timber and plank for the carpenters and coopers, and charcoal for the blacksmith; his cattle, killed for his own consumption and for sale, supplied skins for the tanners, curriers, and shoemakers, and his sheep gave wool and his fields produced cotton and flax for the weavers and spinners, and his orchards fruit for the distiller. His carpenters and sawyers built and kept in repair all the dwelling houses, barns, stables, plows, harrows, gates, etc., on the plantations and the outhouses at the home house. His coopers made the hogsheads the tobacco was prized in and the tight casks to hold the cider and other liquors. The tanners and curriers with the proper vats, etc., tanned and dressed the skins as well for upper as for lower leather to the full amount of the consumption of the estate, and the shoemakers made them into shoes for the Negroes. A professed shoemaker was hired for three or four months in the year to come and make up the shoes for the white part of the family. The blacksmith did all the iron work required by the establishment, as making and repairing plows, harrows, teeth chains, bolts, etc., etc. The spinners, weavers, and knitters made all the coarse cloths and stockings used by the Negroes, and some of finer texture worn by the white family, nearly all worn by the children of it. The distiller made every fall a good deal of apple, peach, and persimmon brandy. The art of distilling from grain was not then among us, and but few public distilleries. All these operations were carried on at the home house, and their results distributed as occasion required to the different plantations. Moreover all the beeves and hogs for consumption or sale were driven up and slaughtered there at the proper seasons, and whatever was to be preserved was salted and packed away for after distribution.

My father kept no steward or clerk about him. He kept his own books and superintended, with the assistance of a trusty slave or two, and occasionally of some of his sons, all the operations at or about the home house above described, except that during the Revolutionary War, and when it was necessary to do a great deal in that way to clothe all his slaves, he had in his service a white man, a weaver of the finer stuffs, to weave himself and superintend the Negro spinning-women. To carry on these operations to the extent required, it will be seen that a considerable force was necessary, besides the house servants, who for such a household, a large family and entertaining a great deal of company, must be numerous — and such a force was constantly kept there, independently of any of the plantations, and besides occasional drafts from them of labor for particular occasions. As I had during my youth constant intercourse with all these people, I remember them all and their several employments as if it was yesterday.

KATE M. ROWLAND, The Life of George Mason

# IV

## White Men and Red

Earliest Known Pictorial Representation of Indians
on American Continents

# 17. John Lawson Visits the Indians of North Carolina

*European readers had an insatiable interest in the Indians of North America. One of the men who tried to satisfy it was the English traveler John Lawson, who arrived in the Southern colonies in 1700, and after a thousand-mile journey among the savages, wrote a book, half of which was devoted to them and their customs. Vivid, sprightly, and accurate, it has been much used by both ethnologists and historians. In it Lawson gave a favorable description of the climate, products, and people of North Carolina. It is sad to record that the Indians whom he celebrated seized him and put him to death in 1711.*

THE INDIANS of North Carolina are a well-shaped, clean-made people, of different statures, as the Europeans are, yet chiefly inclined to be tall. They are a very straight people, and never bend forwards or stoop in the shoulders, unless much overpowered by old age. Their limbs are exceeding well shaped. As for their legs and feet, they are generally the handsomest in the world. Their bodies are a little flat, which is occasioned by being laced hard down to a board in their infancy. This is all the cradle they have, which I shall describe at large elsewhere. Their eyes are black, or of a dark hazel; the white is marbled with red streaks, which is ever common to these people, unless when sprung from a white father or mother. Their color is of a tawny, which would not be so dark did they not daub themselves with bear's oil and a color like burnt cork. This is begun in their infancy and continued for a long time, which fills the pores and enables them better to endure the extremity of the weather. They are never bald on their heads, although never so old, which, I believe, proceeds from their heads being always uncovered, and the greasing their hair, so often as they do, with bear's fat, which is a great nourisher of the hair, and causes it to grow very fast.

Their eyes are commonly full and manly, and their gait sedate and majestic. They never walk backward and forward as we do, nor contemplate on the affairs of loss and gain, the things which daily perplex us. They are dexterous and steady, both as to their hands and feet, to admiration. They will walk over deep brooks and creeks on the smallest poles, and that without any fear or concern. Nay, an Indian will walk on the ridge of a barn or house and look down the gable end, and spit upon the ground as unconcerned as if he was walking on terra firma. In running, leaping, or any such other exercise, their legs seldom miscarry and give them a fall; and as for letting anything fall out of their hands, I never yet knew one example. They are no inventors of any arts or trades worthy mention; the reason of which I take to be that they are not possessed with that care and thoughtfulness, how to provide for the necessaries of life as the Europeans are; yet they will learn anything very soon. I have known an Indian stock guns better than most of our joiners, although he never saw one stocked before; and besides, his working tool was only a sorry knife. I have also known several of them that were slaves to the English, learn handicraft trades very well and speedily. I never saw a dwarf amongst them, nor but one that was humpbacked. Their teeth are yellow with smoking tobacco, which both men and women are much addicted to. They tell us that they had tobacco amongst them before the Europeans made any discovery of that continent. It differs in the leaf from the sweet-scented and oronoco, which are the plants we raise and cultivate in America. Theirs differs likewise much in the smell, when green, from our tobacco before cured. They do not use the same way to cure it as we do, and therefore the difference must be very considerable in taste; for all men (that know tobacco) must allow that it is the ordering thereof which gives a hogo to that weed rather than any natural relish it possesses when green. Although they are great smokers, yet they never are seen to take it in snuff or chew it.

As there are found very few or scarce any deformed or cripples amongst them, so neither did I ever see but one blind man; and then they would give me no account how his blindness came. They had a use for him, which was to lead him with a girl, woman, or boy by a string; so they put what burdens they pleased upon his back and made him very serviceable upon all such occasions. No people have better eyes, or see better in the night or day than the Indians. Some allege that the smoke of the pitch pine which they chiefly burn, does both preserve and strengthen the eyes; as perhaps it may do, because that smoke never offends the eyes, though you hold your face over a great fire thereof. This is occasioned by the volatile part of the turpentine, which rises with the smoke, and is of a friendly, balsamic nature; for the ashes of the pine tree afford no fixed salt in them.

They let their nails grow very long, which, they reckon, is the use nails are designed for, and laugh at the Europeans for paring theirs, which, they say, disarms them of that which Nature designed them for.

They are not of so robust and strong bodies as to lift great burdens and endure labor and slavish work as the Europeans are; yet some that are slaves prove very good and laborious; but, of themselves, they never work as the English do, taking care for no further than what is absolutely necessary to support life. In traveling and hunting they are very indefatigable, because that carries a pleasure along with the profit. I have known some of them very strong; and as for running and leaping, they are extraordinary fellows, and will dance for several nights together with the greatest briskness imaginable, their wind never failing them.

Their dances are of different natures, and for every sort of dance they have a tune, which is allotted for that dance; as, if it be a war dance, they have a warlike song, wherein they express, with all the passion and vehemence imaginable, what they intend to do with their enemies; how they will kill, roast, scalp, beat, and make captive such and such numbers of them; and how many they have destroyed before. All these songs are made new for every feast; nor is one and the same song sung at two several festivals. Some one of the nation (which has the best gift of expressing their designs) is appointed by their king and war captains to make these songs.

Their chiefest game is a sort of arithmetic which is managed by a parcel of small split reeds the thickness of a small bent; these are made very nicely so that they part and are tractable in their hands. They are fifty-one in number, their length about seven inches; when they play, they throw part of them to their antagonist; the art is to discover upon sight how many you have and what you throw to him that plays with you. Some are so expert at their numbers that they will tell ten times together what they throw out of their hands. Although the whole play is carried on with the quickest motion it is possible to use, yet some are so expert at this game as to win great Indian estates by this play. A good set of these reeds, fit to play withal, are valued and sold for a dressed doeskin.

They have several other plays and games, as with the kernels or stones of persimmons, which are in effect the same as our dice, because winning or losing depend on which side appear uppermost and how they happen to fall together.

Another game is managed with a baton and a ball and resembles our trapball; besides, several nations have several games and pastimes which are not used by others.

These savages live in wigwams or cabins built of bark, which are made round like an oven to prevent any damage by hard gales of wind. They make the fire in the middle of the house, and have a hole at the top of the roof right above the fire to let out the smoke. These dwellings are as hot as stoves, where the Indians sleep and sweat all night. The floors thereof are never paved nor swept, so that they have always a loose earth on them. They are often troubled with a multitude of fleas, especially near the places where they dress their deerskins, because that hair harbors them; yet I never felt any ill, unsavory smell in their cabins, whereas, should we live in our houses as they do we should be poisoned with our own nastiness, which confirms these Indians to be, as they really are, some of the sweetest people in the world.

The bark they make their cabins withal is generally cypress, or red or white cedar; and sometimes, when they are a great way from any of these woods, they make use of pine bark, which is the worser sort. In building these fabrics they get very long poles of pine, cedar, hickory, or any other wood that will bend; these are the thickness of the small of a man's leg at the thickest end, which they generally strip of the bark and warm them well in the fire, which makes them tough and fit to bend. Afterwards, they stick the thickest ends of them in the ground about two yards asunder, in a circular form, the distance they design the cabin to be (which is not always round but sometimes oval); then they bend the tops and bring them together, and bind their ends with bark of trees that is proper for that use, as elm is, or sometimes the moss that grows on the trees and is a yard or two long and never rots; then they brace them with other poles to make them strong; afterwards cover them all over with bark, so that they are very warm and tight, and will keep firm against all the weathers that blow. They have other sorts of cabins without windows, which are for their granaries, skins, and merchandises, and others that are covered overhead; the rest left open for the air. These have reed hurdles, like tables, to lie and sit on in summer, and serve for pleasant banqueting houses in the hot season of the year. The cabins they dwell in have benches all round, except where the door stands; on these they lay beasts' skins and mats made of rushes, whereon they sleep and loll. In one of these several families commonly live, though all related to one another.

JOHN LAWSON, History of Carolina

# 18. The Death of King Philip

*Ablest and craftiest of all the New England Indians was Philip, sachem of the Wampanoags. As the white men bought more and more of the Indian land, restricting the tribe to narrower areas and diminished game, unrest grew. Finally in 1675 Philip began the most disastrous Indian war in the history of New England; a war in which twelve towns were destroyed and several thousand whites killed. Hostilities began near Narragansett Bay, but spread through Massachusetts and as far west as the Connecticut River. Before they were ended in the following year the colonists had spent a hundred thousand pounds. Philip's head was long exhibited by the vengeful colonists at Plymouth.*

CAPTAIN CHURCH being now at Plymouth again, weary and worn, would have gone home to his wife and family; but the government being solicitous to engage him in the service until Philip was slain, and promising him satisfaction and redress for some mistreatment that he had met with, he fixes for another expedition.

He had soon volunteers enough to make up the company he desired, and marched through the woods until he came to Pocasset. And not seeing or hearing of any of the enemy, they went over the ferry to Rhode Island, to refresh themselves. The Captain, with about half a dozen in his company, took horses and rid about eight miles down the island to Mr. Sanford's, where they spied two horsemen coming a great pace. Captain Church told his company that "those men (by their riding) come with tidings." When they came up, they proved to be Major Sanford and Captain Golding, who immediately asked Captain Church what he would give to hear some news of Philip. He replied that was what he wanted. They told him they had rid hard with some hopes of overtaking him, and were now come on purpose to inform him that there were just now tidings from Mount Hope. An Indian came down from thence (where Philip's camp now was) and hallooed, and made signs to be fetched over. And being fetched over, he reported that he was fled from Philip, and told them also that Philip was now in Mount Hope Neck. Captain Church thanked them for their good news and said he hoped by tomorrow morning to have the rogue's head. The horses that he and his company came on, standing at the door, his wife must content herself with a short visit, when such game was ahead. They immediately mounted, set spurs to their horses, and away.

The two gentlemen that brought him the tidings told him they would gladly wait upon him to see the event of this expedition. He thanked them, and told them he should be as fond of their company as any men's; and they went with him. And they were soon at Trip's ferry (with Captain Church's company), where the deserter was, who was a fellow of good sense, and told his story handsomely. He offered Captain Church to pilot him to Philip and to help to kill him, that he might revenge his brother's death. Told him that

Philip was now upon a little spot of upland that was in the south end of the miry swamp just at the foot of the mount, which was a spot of ground that Captain Church was well acquainted with.

By that time they were got over the ferry and came near the ground, half the night was spent. The Captain commands a halt, and bringing the company together, he offered Captain Golding that he should have the honor (if he would please accept of it) to beat up Philip's headquarters. He accepted the offer and had his allotted number drawn out to him, and the pilot. Captain Church's instructions to him were to be very careful in his approach to the enemy and be sure not to show himself until by daylight they might see and discern their own men from the enemy; told him also, that his custom in the like cases was to creep with his company on their bellies until they came as near as they could; and that as soon as the enemy discovered them, they would cry out, and that was the word for his men to fire and fall on. He directed him that when the enemy should start and take into the swamp, they should pursue with speed; every man shouting and making what noise he could; for he would give orders to his ambuscade to fire on any that should come silently.

Captain Church, knowing that it was Philip's custom to be foremost in the flight, went down to the swamp, and gave Captain Williams of Scituate the command of the right wing of the ambush, and placed an Englishman and an Indian together behind such shelters of trees etc. as he could find, and took care to place them at such distance that none might pass undiscovered between them; charged them to be careful of themselves, and of hurting their friends, and to fire at any that should come silently through the swamp. But it being somewhat farther through the swamp than he was aware of, he wanted men to make up his ambuscade.

Having placed what men he had, he took Major Sanford by the hand and said, "Sir, I have so placed them that it is scarce possible Philip should escape them." The same moment a shot whistled over their heads, and then the noise of a gun towards Philip's camp. Captain Church at first thought it might be some gun fired by accident; but before he could speak, a whole volley followed, which was earlier than he expected. One of Philip's gang going forth to ease himself, when he had done, looked round him, and Captain

Golding thought that the Indian looked right at him (though probably it was but his conceit); so fired at him; and upon his firing, the whole company that were with him fired upon the enemy's shelter before the Indians had time to rise from their sleep, and so overshot them. But their shelter was open on that side next the swamp, built so on purpose for the convenience of flight on occasion. They were soon in the swamp, and Philip the foremost, who, starting at the first gun, threw his *petunk* and powder horn over his head, catched up his gun and ran as fast as he could scamper, without any more clothes than his small breeches and stockings, and ran directly upon two of Captain Church's ambush. They let him come fair within shot, and the Englishman's gun missing fire, he bid the Indian fire away, and he did so to the purpose; sent one musket bullet through his heart, and another not above two inches from it. He fell upon his face in the mud and water with his gun under him.

By this time the enemy perceived they were waylaid on the east side of the swamp and tacked short about. One of the enemy, who seemed to be a great, surly old fellow, hallooed with a loud voice, and often called out, "*Iootash, Iootash.*" Captain Church called to his Indian, Peter, and asked him who that was that called so. He answered it was old Annawon, Philip's great captain, calling on his soldiers to stand to it and fight stoutly. Now the enemy finding that place of the swamp which was not ambushed, many of them made their escape in the English tracks.

The man that had shot down Philip ran with all speed to Captain Church and informed him of his exploit, who commanded him to be silent about it and let no man more know it until they had driven the swamp clean. But when they had driven the swamp through, and found the enemy had escaped, or at least the most of them, and the sun now up, and so the dew gone that they could not easily track them, the whole company met together at the place where the enemy's night shelter was, and then Captain Church gave them the news of Philip's death. Upon which the whole army gave three loud huzzas. . . .

This being on the last day of the week, the Captain with his company returned to the island, tarried there until Tuesday, and then went off and ranged through all the woods to Plymouth, and received their premium, which was thirty shillings per head, for the enemies which they had killed or taken, instead of all wages; and Philip's head went at the same price. Methinks it is scanty reward and poor encouragement, though it was better than what had been some time before. For this march they received four shillings and sixpence a man, which was all the reward they had, except the honor of killing Philip. This was in the latter end of August, 1676.

THOMAS CHURCH, The History of
King Philip's War

# 19. Mary Rowlandson Is Taken into Captivity

*It was during King Philip's War that Indians who attacked Lancaster, on the Massachusetts frontier, carried away captive a woman of singular resolution, energy, and intellect, with her three children. Mary White Rowlandson, who was probably born in England, was about forty years old at this time, and wife of the first minister of Lancaster. Her courage, physical vigor, and skill in making shirts and stockings for her captors won for her good treatment during the eleven weeks that the savages carried her about in northern Massachusetts and southern New Hampshire. Eventually the influence of John Hoar and a payment of twenty pounds brought her back to her friends. Her Narrative, published in Cambridge in 1682 and immediately reprinted in England, has gone through almost two-score editions. Written in graphic English, it is interesting as an adventure story, a picture of Indian life and character, and a reflection of the religious temper of the Puritan settlers.*

## THE DOLEFUL ONSLAUGHT OF THE INDIANS

ON THE 10th of February, 1675, came the Indians with great numbers upon Lancaster. Their first coming was about sunrising.

Hearing the noise of some guns, we looked out; several houses were burning, and the smoke ascending to heaven. There were five persons taken in one house; the father and the mother and a suckling child they knocked on the head; the other two they took and carried away alive. There were two others, who, being out of their garrison upon some occasion, were set upon; one was knocked on the head, the other escaped. Another there was who, running along, was shot and wounded, and fell down; he begged of them his life, promising them money (as they told me), but they would not hearken to him, but knocked him in the head, and stripped him naked, and split open his bowels. Another seeing many of the Indians about his barn ventured and went out, but was quickly shot down. There were three others belonging to the same garrison who were killed; the Indians, getting up upon the roof of the barn, had advantage to shoot down upon them over their fortification. Thus these murderous wretches went on burning and destroying before them.

At length they came and beset our own house, and quickly it was the dolefulest day that ever mine eyes saw. The house stood upon the edge of a hill; some of the Indians got behind the hill, others into the barn, and others behind anything that could shelter them; from all which places they shot against the house, so that the bullets seemed to fly like hail, and quickly they wounded one man among us, then another, and then a third. About two hours (according to my observation in that amazing time) they had been about the house before they prevailed to fire it (which they did with flax and hemp which they brought out of the barn, and there being no defense about the house, only two flankers at two opposite corners, and one of them not finished); they fired it once, and one ventured out and quenched it, but they quickly fired it again, and that took. Now is the dreadful hour come that I have often heard of (in time of the war, as it was the case of others), but now mine eyes see it. Some in our house were fighting for their lives, others wallowing in their blood, the house on fire over our heads, and the bloody heathen ready to knock us on the head if we stirred out. Now might we hear mothers and children crying out for themselves and one another, "Lord, what shall we do!" Then I took my children (and one of my sisters hers) to go forth and leave the house, but, as soon as we came to the door and appeared, the Indians shot so thick that the bullets rattled against the house as if one had taken a handful of stones and threw them, so that we were forced to give back. We had six stout dogs belonging to our garrison, but none of them would stir, though another time if any Indian had come to the door, they were ready to fly upon him and tear him down. The Lord hereby would make us the more to acknowledge His hand, and to see that our help is always in Him. But out we must go, the fire increasing, and coming along behind us roaring, and the Indians gaping before us with their guns, spears, and hatchets to devour us. No sooner were we out of the house but my brother-in-law (being before wounded in defending the house, in or near the throat) fell down dead, whereat the Indians scornfully shouted and hallooed, and were presently upon him, stripping off his clothes. The bullets flying thick, one went through my side, and the same (as would seem) through the bowels and hand of my dear child in my arms. One of my elder sister's children (named William) had then his leg broke, which the Indians perceiving they knocked him on the head. Thus were we butchered by those merciless heathen, standing amazed, with the blood running down to our heels. My eldest sister being yet in the house, and seeing those woeful sights, the infidels hauling mothers one way and children another, and some wallowing in their blood; and her elder son telling her that her son William was dead, and myself was wounded, she said, "And, Lord, let me die with them"; which was no sooner said, but she was struck with a bullet, and fell down dead over the threshold. I hope she is reaping the fruit of her good labors, being faithful to the service of God in her place.

I had often before this said, that if the Indians should come, I should choose rather to be killed by them than taken alive, but when it came to the trial, my mind changed; their glittering weapons so daunted my spirit, that I chose rather to go along with those (as I may say) ravenous bears, than that moment to end my days. And that I may the better declare what happened to me during that grievous captivity, I shall particularly speak of the several removes we had up and down the wilderness.

## THE FIRST REMOVE

Now away we must go with those barbarous creatures, with our bodies wounded and bleeding, and our hearts no less than our bodies. About a mile we went that night, up upon a hill, within sight of the town, where they intended to lodge. There was hard by a vacant house (deserted by the English before, for fear of the Indians). I asked them whether I might not lodge in the house that night, to which they answered, "What, will you love Englishmen still?" This was the dolefulest night that ever my eyes saw. Oh, the roaring and singing, and dancing, and yelling of those black creatures in the night, which made the place a lively resemblance of hell. And as miserable was the waste that was there made, of horses, cattle, sheep, swine, calves, lambs, roasting pigs, and fowl (which they had plundered in the town), some roasting, some lying and burning, and some boiling, to feed our merciless enemies, who were joyful enough, though we were disconsolate. To add to the dolefulness of the former day and the dismalness of the present night, my thoughts ran upon my losses and sad, bereaved condition. All was gone, my husband gone (at least separated from me, he being in the Bay; and to add to my grief, the Indians told me they would kill him as he came homeward), my children gone, my relations and friends gone, our house and home, and all our comforts within door and without, all was gone (except my life), and I knew not but the next moment that might go too.

There remained nothing to me but one poor, wounded babe, and it seemed at present worse than death, that it was in such a pitiful condition, bespeaking compassion, and I had no refreshing for it, nor suitable things to revive it. Little do many think what is the savageness and brutishness of this barbarous enemy, — aye, even those that seem to profess more than others among them — when the English have fallen into their hands.

## THE SECOND REMOVE

But now (the next morning) I must turn my back upon the town, and travel with them into the vast and desolate wilderness, I knew not whither. It is not my tongue or pen can express the sorrows of my heart, and bitterness of my spirit, that I had at this departure; but God was with me in a wonderful manner, carrying me along and bearing up my spirit, that it did not quite fail. One of the Indians carried my poor wounded babe upon a horse; it went moaning all along, "I shall die, I shall die." I went on foot after it, with sorrow that cannot be expressed. At length I took it off the horse, and carried it in my arms, till my strength failed and I fell down with it. Then they set me upon a horse with my wounded child in my lap, and there being no furniture on the horse's back, as we were going down a steep hill, we both fell over the horse's head, at which they, like inhuman creatures, laughed, and rejoiced to see it, though I thought we should there have ended our days, as overcome with so many difficulties. But the Lord renewed my strength still, and carried me along, that I might see more of His power, yea, so much that I could never have thought of, had I not experienced it.

After this it quickly began to snow, and when night came on they stopped; and now down I must sit in the snow by a little fire, and a few boughs behind me, with my sick child in my lap and calling much for water, being now (through the wound) fallen into a violent fever. My own wound also growing so stiff that I could scarce sit down or rise up, yet so it must be, that I must sit all this cold winter night, upon the cold snowy ground, with my sick child in my arms, looking that every hour would be the last of its life; and having no Christian friend near me, either to comfort or help me. Oh, I may see the wonderful power of God, that my spirit did not utterly sink under my affliction; still the Lord upheld me with His gracious and merciful spirit, and we were both alive to see the light of the next morning.

## THE THIRD REMOVE

Thus nine days I sat upon my knees with my babe in my lap, till my flesh was raw again. My child being even ready to depart this sorrowful world, they bade me carry it out to another wigwam (I suppose because they would not be troubled with such spectacles), whither I went with a very heavy heart and down I sat with the picture of death in my lap. About two hours in the night, my sweet babe like a lamb departed this life, on February 18, 1675, it being about six years and five months old. It was nine days from the first wounding in this miserable condition, without any refreshing of one nature or other, except a little cold water. I cannot but take notice how at another time I could not bear to be in the room where any dead person was, but now the case is changed. I must and could lie down by my dead babe, side by side all the night after. I have thought since of the wonderful goodness of God to me in preserving me in the use of my reason and senses in that distressed time, that I did not use wicked and violent means to end my own miserable life.

In the morning when they understood that my child was dead they sent for me home to my master's wigwam (by my master in this writing must be understood Quanopin, who was a Sagamore, and married King Philip's wife's sister; not that he first took me, but I was sold to him by another Narraganset Indian, who took me when first I came out of the garrison). I went to take up my dead child in my arms to carry it with me, but they bid me let it alone. There was no resisting, but go I must and leave it. When I had been at my master's wigwam, I took the first opportunity I could get to go look after my dead child. When I came I asked them what they had done with it. Then they told me it was upon the hill. Then they went and showed me where it was, where I saw the ground was newly digged, and there they told me they had buried it. There I left that child in the wilderness, and must commit it and myself also in this wilderness condition to Him who is above all. God having taken away this dear child, I went to see my daughter Mary, who was at this same Indian town, at a wigwam not very far off, though we had little liberty or opportunity to see one another. She was about ten years old, and taken from the door at first by a praying Indian and sold afterward for a gun. When I came in sight, she would fall a-weeping, at which they were provoked and would not let me come near her, but bade me be gone, which was a heart-cutting word to me. I had one child dead, another in the wilderness, I knew not where; the third they would not let come near to me.

So I took my leave of them, and in coming along my heart melted into tears, more than all the while I was with them, and I was almost swallowed up with the thoughts that ever I should go home again. About the sun's going down, Mr. Hoar, myself, and the two Indians, came to Lancaster, and a solemn sight it was to me. There had I lived many comfortable years amongst my relations and neighbors; and now not one Christian to be seen, nor one house left standing. We went on to a farmhouse that was yet standing, where we lay all night; and a comfortable lodging we had, though nothing but straw to lie on. The Lord preserved us in safety that night, and raised us up again in the morning, and carried us along, that before noon we came to Concord. Now was I full of joy and yet not without sorrow — joy to see such a lovely sight, so many Christians together, and some of them my neighbors. There I met with my brother and my brother-in-law, who asked me if I knew where his wife was. Poor heart! he had helped to bury her and knew it not; she, being shot down by the house, was partly burned, so that those who were at Boston at the desolation of the town and came back afterward and buried the dead did not know her. Yet I was not without sorrow, to think how many were looking and longing, and my own children amongst the rest, to enjoy that deliverance that I had now received; and I did not know whether ever I should see them again. Being recruited with food and raiment, we went to Boston that day, where I met with my dear husband; but the thoughts of our dear children, one being dead and the other we could not tell where, abated our comfort each to other.

MARY ROWLANDSON, Narrative

# 20. John Giles Is Captured by the Indians

*King William's War against the French and Indians brought fresh sufferings upon the English settlers. In lower New Hampshire in 1689 the savages slew Thomas Giles, who had been chief justice of the county of Cornwall under the government of the Duke of York, and carried off his son John. The latter lived to become author of one of the most famous narratives of Indian captivity, and Indian interpreter for the Massachusetts government.*

ON THE second day of August, 1689, in the morning, my honored father, Thomas Giles, Esq., went with some laborers, my two elder brothers, and myself, to one of his farms which lay upon the river about three miles above Fort Charles, adjoining Pemmaquid Falls, there to gather in his English harvest, and we labored securely till noon. After we had dined, our people went to their labor, some in one field to their English hay, the others to another field of English corn. My father, the youngest of my two brothers, and myself tarried near the farmhouse in which we had dined till about one of the clock, at which time we heard the report of several great guns at the fort. Upon which my father said he hoped it was a signal of good news, and that the great council had sent back the soldiers to cover the inhabitants (for on report of the revolution they had deserted). But to our great surprise, about thirty or forty Indians, at that moment, discharged a volley of shot at us from behind a rising ground, near our barn. The yelling of the Indians, the whistling of their shot, and the voice of my father, whom I heard cry out, "What now! what now!" so terrified me (though he seemed to be handling a gun) that I endeavored to make my escape. My brother ran one way and I another, and, looking over my shoulder, I saw a stout fellow, painted, pursuing me with a gun, and a cutlass glittering in his hand which I expected every moment in my brains. I soon fell down, and the Indian seized me by the left hand. He offered me no abuse, but tied my arms, then lifted me up and pointed to the place where the people were at work about the hay and led me that way. As we went, we crossed where my father was, who looked very pale and bloody, and walked very slowly. When we came to the place, I saw two men shot down on the flats, and one or two more knocked on their heads with hatchets, crying out "O Lord!" etc. There the Indians brought two captives, one a man, and my brother James, who, with me had endeavored to escape by running from the house when we were first attacked.

After doing what mischief they could, they sat down and made us sit with them. After some time, we arose, and the Indians pointed for us to go eastward. We marched about a quarter of a mile, and then made a halt. Here they brought my father to us. They made proposals to him, by old Moxus, who told him that those were strange Indians who shot him, and that he was sorry for it. My father replied that he was a dying man, and wanted no favor of them but to pray with his children. This being granted him, he recommended us to the protection and blessing of God Almighty, then gave us the best advice, and took his leave of this life, hoping in God that we should meet in a better. He parted with a cheerful voice, but looked very pale, by reason of his great loss of blood, which now gushed out of his shoes. The Indians led him aside! — I heard the blows of the hatchet, but neither shriek nor groan! I afterwards heard that he had five or seven shot holes through his waistcoat or jacket and that he was covered with some boughs.

The Indians led us, their captives, on the east side of the river, towards the fort, and when we came within a mile and a half of the fort and town and could see the fort, we saw fire and smoke on all sides. Here we made a short stop, and then moved, within or near the distance of three-quarters of a mile from the fort, into a thick swamp. There I saw my mother and my two little sisters and many other captives who were taken from the town. My mother asked me about my father. I told her he was killed, but could say no more for grief. She burst into tears, and the Indians moved me a little farther off, and seized me with cords to a tree.

JOHN GILES, Memoirs of Odd Adventures

# 21. James Smith Is Adopted by the Delawares

*The pioneer James Smith, of the sturdy Ulster Scottish stock which contributed so much to the making of America, was only about eighteen years old when, having left his frontier home in Pennsylvania to help build a military road from Shippensburg, Pa., to the Youghiogheny River, he was captured by the Indian allies of the French. Death by torture confronted him, but he was saved by being adopted into an Indian family. It was only after four years of wanderings through the wilderness of Ohio and Canada that he escaped near Montreal in 1759, and made his way to territory under the British flag. After the end of the Revolutionary War he became one of the leading citizens of Kentucky, well known for his political and religious activities. He was a good warrior with both pen and sword, fighting the Shaker sect by pamphlets as he had repeatedly fought the Indians with blade and musket. But he is best remembered for his vivid story of his adoption and captivity, published in Kentucky in 1799.*

IN MAY, 1755, the province of Pennsylvania agreed to send out three hundred men in order to cut a wagon road from Fort Loudon to join Braddock's road, near the Turkey Foot, or three forks of Yohogania. My brother-in-law, William Smith, Esq., of Conococheague, was appointed commissioner to have the oversight of these road cutters. . . .

We went on with the road without interruption until near the Allegheny Mountain, when I was sent back in order to hurry up some provision wagons that were on the way after us. I proceeded down the road as far as the crossings of Juniata, where, finding the wagons were coming on as fast as possible, I returned up the road again towards the Allegheny Mountain, in company with one Arnold Vigoras. About four or five miles above Bedford, three Indians had made a blind of bushes, stuck in the ground as though they grew naturally, where they concealed themselves about fifteen yards from the road. When we came opposite to them, they fired upon us, at this short distance, and killed my fellow traveler, yet their bullets did not touch me; but my horse, making a violent start, threw me, and the Indians immediately ran up and took me prisoner. The one that laid hold on me was a Canafatauga; the other two were Delawares. One of them could speak English and asked me if there were any more white men coming after. I told them not any near that I knew of. Two of these Indians stood by me whilst the other scalped my comrade; then they set off and ran at a smart rate through the woods for about fifteen miles, and that night we slept on the Allegheny Mountain, without fire.

The next morning they divided the last of their provision which they had brought from Fort Duquesne and gave me an equal share, which was about two or three ounces of moldy biscuit — this and a young ground hog, about as large as a rabbit, roasted and also equally divided, was all the provision we had until we came to the Loyal Hannan, which was about fifty miles; and a great part of the way we came through exceeding rocky laurel thickets without any path. When we came to the west side of Laurel Hill, they gave the scalp halloo, as usual, which is a long yell or halloo for every scalp or prisoner they have in possession; the last of these scalp halloos was followed with quick and sudden, shrill shouts of joy and triumph.

As I was at this time unacquainted with this mode of firing and yelling of the savages, I concluded that there were thousands of Indians there, ready to receive General Braddock; but what added to my surprise, I saw numbers running towards me, stripped naked, excepting breechclouts, and painted in the most hideous manner, of various colors, though the principal color was vermilion or a bright red; yet there was annexed to this, black, brown, blue, etc. As they approached, they formed themselves into two long ranks, about two or three rods apart. I was told by an Indian that could speak English that I must run betwixt these ranks, and that they would flog me all the way as I ran, and if I ran quick it would be so much the better, as they would quit when I got to the end of the ranks. There appeared to be a general rejoicing around me, yet I could find nothing like joy in my breast; but I started to the race with all the resolution and vigor I was capable of exerting, and found that it was as I had been told, for I was flogged the whole way. When I had got near the end of the lines, I was struck with something that appeared to me to be a stick or the handle of a tomahawk, which caused me to fall to the ground. On my recovering my senses, I endeavored to renew my race, but as I arose, someone cast sand in my eyes, which blinded me so that I could not see where to run. They continued beating me most intolerably until I was at length insensible. But before I lost my senses, I remember my wishing them to strike the fatal blow, for I thought they intended killing me but apprehended they were too long about it.

The first thing I remember was my being in the fort, amidst the

French and Indians, and a French doctor standing by me, who had opened a vein in my left arm; after which the interpreter asked me how I did. I told him I felt much pain; the doctor then washed my wounds and the bruised places of my body with French brandy. As I felt faint and the brandy smelt well, I asked for some inwardly, but the doctor told me, by the interpreter, that it did not suit my case. I was then sent to the hospital and carefully attended by the doctors, and recovered quicker than what I expected.

Some time after I was there, I was visited by the Delaware Indian already mentioned who was at the taking of me and could speak some English. Though he spoke but bad English, yet I found him to be a man of considerable understanding. I asked him if I had done anything that had offended the Indians which caused them to treat me so unmercifully. He said no, it was only an old custom the Indians had, and it was like how-do-you-do; after that, he said, I would be well used. I asked him if I should be admitted to return with the French. He said no — and told me that as soon as I recovered, I must not only go with the Indians, but must be made an Indian myself. I asked him what news from Braddock's army. He said the Indians spied them every day, and he showed me by making marks on the ground with a stick that Braddock's army was advancing in very close order and that the Indians would surround them, take trees, and (as he expressed it) "shoot um down all one pigeon."

Some time after this, I heard a number of scalp halloos and saw a company of Indians and French coming in. I observed they had a great many bloody scalps, grenadiers' caps, British canteens, bayonets, etc. with them. They brought the news that Braddock was defeated. After that another company came in which appeared to be about one hundred, and chiefly Indians, and it seemed to me that almost every one of this company was carrying scalps; after this came another company with a number of wagon horses, and also a great many scalps. Those that were coming in, and those that had arrived, kept a constant firing of small arms, and also the great guns in the fort, which were accompanied with the most hideous shouts and yells from all quarters; so that it appeared to me as if the infernal regions had broke loose.

About sundown, I beheld a small party coming in with about a dozen prisoners, stripped naked, with their hands tied behind their backs, and their faces and part of their bodies blacked — these prisoners they burned to death on the bank of the Allegheny River opposite to the fort. I stood on the fort wall until I beheld them begin to burn one of these men; they had him tied to a stake and kept touching him with firebrands, red-hot irons, etc., and he screaming in a most doleful manner, the Indians in the meantime yelling like infernal spirits. As this scene appeared too shocking for me to behold, I retired to my lodging, both sore and sorry. . . .

A few days after this the Indians demanded me and I was obliged to go with them. I was not yet well able to march, but they took me in a canoe up the Allegheny River to an Indian town that was on the north side of the river, about forty miles above Fort Duquesne. Here I remained about three weeks, and was then taken to an Indian town on the west branch of Muskingum, about twenty miles above the forks, which was called Tullihas, inhabited by Delawares, Caughnewagas, and Mohicans.

The day after my arrival at the aforesaid town, a number of Indians collected about me, and one of them began to pull the hair out of my head. He had some ashes on a piece of bark in which he frequently dipped his fingers in order to take the firmer hold, and so he went on, as if he had been plucking a turkey, until he had all the hair clean out of my head, except a small spot about three or four inches square on my crown; this they cut off with a pair of scissors, excepting three locks, which they dressed up in their own mode. Two of these they wrapped round with a narrow beaded garter made by themselves for that purpose, and the other they plaited at full length and then stuck it full of silver brooches. After this they bored my nose and ears, and fixed me off with earrings and nose jewels; then they ordered me to strip off my clothes and put on a breechclout, which I did; then they painted my head, face, and body in various colors. They put a large belt of wampum on my neck, and silver bands on my hands and right arm; and so an old chief led me out in the street and gave the alarm halloo, *oo-wigh,* several times repeated quick, and on this, all that were in the town came running and stood round the old chief, who held me by the hand in the midst. As I at that time knew nothing of their mode of adoption, and had seen them put to death all they had taken, and as I never could find that they saved a man alive at Braddock's defeat, I made no doubt but they were about putting me to death in some cruel manner. The old chief, holding me by the hand, made a long speech, very loud, and when he had done he handed me to three young squaws, who led me by the hand down the bank into the river until the water was up to our middle. The squaws then made signs to me to plunge myself into the water, but I did not understand them; I thought that the result of the council was that I should be drowned, and that these young ladies were to be the executioners. They all three laid violent hold of me, and I for some time opposed them with all my might, which occasioned loud laughter by the multitude that were on the bank of the river. At length, one of the squaws made out to speak a little English (for I believe they began to be afraid of me) and said, "No hurt you"; on this, I gave myself up to their ladyships, who were as good as their word, for though they plunged me under water and washed and rubbed me severely, yet I could not say they hurt me much.

These young women then led me up to the council house, where some of the tribe were ready with new clothes for me. They gave me a new, ruffled shirt, which I put on, also a pair of leggings done off with ribbons and beads, likewise a pair of moccasins, and garters dressed with beads, porcupine quills, and red hair — also a tinsel-laced cap. They again painted my head and face with various colors, and tied a bunch of red feathers to one of these locks they had left on the crown of my head, which stood up five or six inches. They seated me on a bearskin, and gave me a pipe, tomahawk, and pole-catskin pouch, which had been skinned pocket fashion, and contained tobacco, killegenico or dry sumach leaves, which they mix with their tobacco, also spunk, flint, and steel. When I was thus seated, the Indians came in dressed and painted in their grandest manner. As they came in they took their seats and for a considerable time there was a profound silence; every one was smoking, but not a word was spoken among them. At length one of the chiefs made a speech which was delivered to me by an interpreter, and was as followeth: "My son, you are now flesh of our flesh and bone of our bone."

Account of the Remarkable Occurrences in the Life
and Travels of Colonel James Smith

# V

## The Struggle for the Continent

The Taking of Quebec

# 22. George Washington Warns Off the French

*One October morning in 1753, a young Virginian rode off, quite innocently, upon an errand that was to mark the virtual beginning of the Seven Years' War in America — the war which decided that an English and not a French civilization should dominate the continent. The French were building forts along the Ohio. Settlers sent out by the Ohio Company were being killed by the Indians or taken prisoners by the French. Governor Dinwiddie of Virginia determined to send Washington, in the King's name, to tell the French Commandant that his invasion had aroused "surprise and concern," and that he must withdraw from British soil. At Fort Le Bœuf the young major of Virginia militia was rebuffed by the French officer in charge. But he brought back valuable information about the French intentions and strength; and Dinwiddie, forwarding this report to London, saw to it that he was promoted to be lieutenant-colonel. A little later he was busy enlisting and drilling men for service against these French trespassers. One of the greatest of American careers had fully opened.*

WEDNESDAY, October 31, 1753. — I was commissioned and appointed by the Honorable Robert Dinwiddie, Esq., Governor etc. of Virginia, to visit and deliver a letter to the commandant of the French forces on the Ohio, and set out on the intended journey the same day. The next I arrived at Fredericksburg, and engaged Mr. Jacob Vanbraam to be my French interpreter, and proceeded with him to Alexandria, where we provided necessaries. From thence we went to Winchester, and got baggage, horses, etc., and from thence we pursued the new road to Wills Creek, where we arrived the 14th of November. . . .

Shingiss [Delaware chief] attended us to the Loggs Town, where we arrived between sunsetting and dark, the 25th day after I left Williamsburg. We traveled over some extreme good and bad land to get to this place.

As soon as I came into town, I went to Monacatootha (as the Half-King was out at his hunting cabin on Little Beaver Creek, about fifteen miles off) and informed him by John Davison, my Indian interpreter, that I was sent a messenger to the French general, and was ordered to call upon the sachems of the Six Nations to acquaint them with it. I gave him a string of wampum and a twist of tobacco, and desired him to send for the Half-King, which he promised to do by a runner in the morning, and for other sachems. I invited him and the other great men present to my tent, where they stayed about an hour and returned.

[November] 25th. — I inquired into the situation of the French on the Mississippi — their number, and what forts they had built. They informed me that there were four small forts between New Orleans and the Black Islands garrisoned with about thirty or forty men, and a few small pieces in each.

About three o'clock this evening the Half-King came to town. I went up and invited him privately to my tent and desired him to relate some of the particulars of his journey to the French commandant, and reception there, also to give me an account of the ways and distance. He told me that the nearest and levelest way was now impassable, by reason of many large, miry savannas; that we must be obliged to go by Venango, and should not get to the near fort under five or six nights' sleep, good traveling. When he went to the fort, he said, he was received in a very stern manner by the late commander, who asked him very abruptly what he had come about and to declare his business.

26th. — As I had orders to make all possible dispatch, and waiting here was very contrary to my inclinations, I thanked him in the most suitable manner I could, and told him that my business required the greatest expedition and would not admit of that delay. He was not well pleased that I should offer to go before the time he had appointed, and told me that he could not consent to our going without a guard for fear some accident should befall us and draw a reflection upon him. And accordingly he gave orders to

King Shingiss, who was present, to attend on Wednesday night with the wampum, and two men of their nation to be in readiness to set out with us next morning. As I found it was impossible to get off without affronting them in the most egregious manner, I consented to stay.

30th. — Last night the great men assembled to their council house to consult further about this journey, and who were to go; the result of which was that only three of their chiefs with one of their best hunters should be our convoy.

We set out about nine o'clock with the Half-King Jeskakake, White Thunder, and the hunter, and traveled on the road to Venango, where we arrived the 4th of December without anything remarkable happening but a continued series of bad weather.

We found the French colors hoisted at a house from which they had driven Mr. John Frazier, an English subject. I immediately repaired to it to know where the commander resided. There were three officers, one of whom, Captain Joncaire, informed me that he had the command of the Ohio, but that there was a general officer at the near fort, where he advised me to apply for an answer. He invited us to sup with them, and treated us with the greatest complaisance.

The wine, as they dosed themselves pretty plentifully with it, soon banished the restraint which at first appeared in their conversation, and gave a license to their tongues to reveal their sentiments more freely.

They told me that it was their absolute design to take possession of the Ohio, and, by G —, they would do it. For that, although they were sensible the English could raise two men for their one, yet they knew their motions were too slow and dilatory to prevent any undertaking of theirs. They pretend to have an undoubted right to the river from a discovery made by one La Salle sixty years ago, and the rise of this expedition is to prevent our settling on the river or waters of it, as they had heard of some families moving out in order thereto.

[December] 5th. — Rained excessively all day, which prevented our traveling.

6th. — The Half-King came to my tent, quite sober, and insisted very much that I should stay and hear what he had to say to the

French. I fain would have prevented his speaking anything till he came to the commandant, but could not prevail. He told me that at this place a council fire was kindled, where all their business with these people was to be transacted, and that the management of the Indian affairs was left solely to Monsieur Joncaire. As I was desirous of knowing the issue of this, I agreed to stay.

About ten o'clock they met in council. The king spoke much the same as he had before done to the general, and offered the French speech belt, which had before been demanded, with the marks of four towns on it, which Monsieur Joncaire refused to receive, but desired him to carry it to the fort of the commander.

7th. — At eleven o'clock we set out for the fort, and were prevented from arriving there till the 11th by excessive rains, snows, and bad traveling through many mires and swamps. These we were obliged to pass to avoid crossing the creek, which was impassable either by fording or rafting, the water was so high and rapid.

12th. — I prepared early to wait upon the commander, and was received and conducted to him by the second officer in command. I acquainted him with my business, and offered my commission and letter.

13th. — The chief officers retired to hold a council of war, which gave me an opportunity of taking the dimensions of the fort and making what observations I could.

I could get no certain account of the number of men here, but, according to the best judgment I could form, there are an hundred exclusive of officers, of which there are many. I also gave orders to the people who were with me to take an exact account of the canoes which were hauled up to convey their forces down in the spring. This they did, and told fifty of birchbark and one hundred and seventy of pine, besides many others which were blocked out in readiness to make.

14th. — As I found many plots concerted to retard the Indians' business and prevent their returning with me, I endeavored all that lay in my power to frustrate their schemes and hurry them on to execute their intended design. They accordingly pressed for admittance this evening, which at length was granted them, privately, with the commander and one or two other officers. The Half-King told me that he offered the wampum to the commander, who evaded taking it, and made many fair promises of love and friendship; said he wanted to live in peace and trade amicably with them, as a proof of which he would send some goods immediately down to the Loggs Town for them. But I rather think the design of that is to bring away all our straggling traders they meet with, as I privately understood they intended to carry an officer etc., with them. And what rather confirms this opinion — I was inquiring of the commander by what authority he had made prisoners of several of our English subjects. He told me that the country belonged to them; that no Englishman had a right to trade upon those waters; and that he had orders to make every person prisoner who attempted it on the Ohio, or the waters of it.

15th. — The commandant ordered a plentiful store of liquor, provision, etc., to be put on board our canoe, and appeared to be extremely complaisant though he was exerting every artifice which he could invent to set our own Indians at variance with us, to prevent their going till after our departure — presents, rewards, and everything which could be suggested by him or his officers. I can't say that ever in my life I suffered so much anxiety as I did in this affair. I saw that every stratagem which the most fruitful brain could invent was practised to win the Half-King to their interest, and that leaving him here was giving them the opportunity they aimed at.

As I was very much pressed by the Indians to wait this day for them, I consented, on a promise that nothing should hinder them in the morning.

16th. — The French were not slack in their inventions to keep the Indians this day also, but as they were obligated according to promise to give the present, they then endeavored to try the power of liquor, which I doubt not would have prevailed at any other time than this. But I urged and insisted with the Half-King so closely upon his word that he refrained and set off with us as he had engaged.

23d. — Our horses were now so weak and feeble and the baggage so heavy (as we were obliged to provide all the necessaries which the journey would require) that we doubted much their performing it. Therefore, myself and others (except the drivers, who were obliged to ride) gave up our horses for packs to assist along with the baggage. I put myself in an Indian walking dress, and con-tinued with them three days till I found there was no probability of their getting home in any reasonable time. The horses grew less able to travel every day; the cold increased very fast; and the roads were becoming much worse by a deep snow, continually freezing. Therefore, as I was uneasy to get back to make report of my pro-ceedings to his Honor the Governor, I determined to prosecute my journey the nearest way through the woods on foot.

Accordingly I left Mr. Vanbraam in charge of our baggage, with money and directions to provide necessaries from place to place for themselves and horses, and to make the most convenient dispatch in traveling.

I took my necessary papers, pulled off my clothes, and tied myself up in a matchcoat. Then with gun in hand and pack at my back, in which were my papers and provisions, I set out with Mr. Gist, fitted in the same manner, on Wednesday the 26th.

The day following, just after we had passed a place called the Murdering Town, we fell in with a party of French Indians who had lain in wait for us. One of them fired at Mr. Gist or me, not fifteen steps off, but fortunately missed. We took this fellow into custody and kept him till about nine o'clock, then let him go, and walked all the remaining part of the night without making any stop, that we might get the start so far as to be out of the reach of their pursuit the next day, since we were well assured that they would follow our track as soon as it was light. The next day we continued traveling till quite dark and got to the river about two miles above Shannapins. We expected to have found the river frozen, but it was not, only about fifty yards from each shore. The ice, I suppose, had broken up above, for it was driving in vast quantities.

There was no way for getting over but on a raft, which we set about with but one poor hatchet and finished just after sunsetting. This was a whole day's work. Then set off. But before we were halfway over, we were jammed in the ice in such a manner that we expected every moment our raft to sink and ourselves to perish.

Tuesday, the 1st day of January, we left Mr. Frazier's house and arrived at Mr. Gist's at Monongahela the 2d, where I bought a horse, saddle, etc. The 6th we met seventeen horses loaded with materials and stores for a fort at the forks of the Ohio, and the day after some families going out to settle. This day we arrived at Wills Creek, after as fatiguing a journey as it is possible to conceive, rendered so by excessive bad weather. From the 1st day of December to the 15th there was but one day on which it did not rain or snow incessantly; and throughout the whole journey we met with nothing but one continued series of cold, wet weather, which occasioned very uncomfortable lodgings, especially after we had quitted our tent, which was some screen from the inclemency of it.

On the 11th I got to Belvoir, where I stopped one day to take necessary rest, and then set out and arrived in Williamsburg the 16th, when I waited upon his Honor the Governor with the letter I had brought from the French commandant, and to give an account of the success of my proceedings. This I beg leave to do by offering the foregoing narrative, as it contains the most remarkable occurrences which happened in my journey.

The Writings of George Washington

# 23. Franklin Supplies Wagons for General Braddock

*The Virginia militia were of course unable to check the French in the West, though at Fort Necessity Washington heard the bullets whistle, and wrote that he liked the sound. It was decided in London to send over an expeditionary force under the sixty-year-old General Edward Braddock. This force suffered in America from administrative confusion and lack of resources. The Quaker and German farmers of Pennsylvania selfishly refused to aid it until Franklin intervened, engaging to procure horses and wagons, and bringing in all that were needed. In the end he lost money and reputation by his patriotic but unfortunate service. This fact may have prejudiced his recollections of Braddock. In July, 1755, that brave though boastful officer led two gallant British regiments and a large number of Americans across the Monongahela on a terrible march to disaster and death.*

IN CONVERSATION with him one day he was giving me some account of his intended progress. "After taking Fort Duquesne," says he, "I am to proceed to Niagara; and, having taken that, to Frontenac, if the season will allow time, and I suppose it will, for Duquesne can hardly detain me above three or four days; and then I see nothing that can obstruct my march to Niagara." Having before revolved in my mind the long line his army must make in their march by a very narrow road, to be cut for them through the woods and bushes, and also what I had read of a former defeat of fifteen hundred French, who invaded the Iroquois country, I had conceived some doubts and some fears for the event of the campaign. But I ventured only to say: "To be sure, sir, if you arrive well before Duquesne with these fine troops, so well provided with artillery, that place, not yet completely fortified, and, as we hear, with no very strong garrison, can probably make but a short resistance. The only danger I apprehend of obstruction to your march is from ambuscades of Indians, who, by constant practice, are dexterous in laying and executing them; and the slender line, near four miles long, which your army must make, may expose it to be attacked by surprise in its flanks, and to be cut like a thread into several pieces, which, from their distance, cannot come up in time to support each other."

He smiled at my ignorance, and replied: "These savages may, indeed, be a formidable enemy to your raw American militia, but upon the King's regular and disciplined troops, sir, it is impossible they should make any impression." I was conscious of an impropriety in my disputing with a military man in matters of his profession, and said no more. The enemy, however, did not take the advantage of his army which I apprehended its long line of march exposed it to, but let it advance without interruption till within nine miles of the place; and then, when more in a body (for it had just passed a river where the front had halted till all had come over), and in a more open part of the woods than any it had passed, attacked its advance guard by a heavy fire from behind trees and bushes, which was the first intelligence the general had of an enemy's being near him. This guard being disordered, the general hurried the troops up to their assistance, which was done in great confusion, through wagons, baggage, and cattle; and presently the fire came upon their flank. The officers, being on horseback, were more easily distinguished, picked out as marks, and fell very fast; and the soldiers were crowded together in a huddle, having or hearing no orders, and standing to be shot at till two-thirds of them were killed; and then, being seized with a panic, the whole fled with precipitation.

The wagoners took each a horse out of his team, and scampered; their example was immediately followed by others, so that all the wagons, provisions, artillery, and stores were left to the enemy. The general, being wounded, was brought off with difficulty; his secretary, Mr. Shirley, was killed by his side; and out of eighty-six officers, sixty-three were killed or wounded, and seven hundred and fourteen men killed out of eleven hundred. These eleven hundred had been picked men from the whole army; the rest had been left behind with Colonel Dunbar, who was to follow with the heavier part of the stores, provisions, and baggage. The flyers, not being pursued, arrived at Dunbar's camp, and the panic they brought with them instantly seized him and all his people; and though he had now above one thousand men, and the enemy who had beaten Braddock did not at most exceed four hundred Indians and French together, instead of proceeding and endeavoring to recover some of the lost honor, he ordered all the stores, ammunition, etc., to be destroyed, that he might have more horses to assist his flight toward the settlements and less lumber to remove. He was there met with requests from the governors of Virginia, Maryland, and Pennsylvania, that he would post his troops on the frontiers so as to afford some protection to the inhabitants; but he continued his hasty march through all the country, not thinking himself safe till he arrived at Philadelphia, where the inhabitants could protect him. This whole transaction gave us Americans the first suspicion that our exalted ideas of the prowess of British regulars had not been well founded.

The Autobiography of Benjamin Franklin

# 24. Montcalm and Wolfe Fight on the Heights of Abraham

*The capture of Quebec meant the conquest of Canada. William Pitt, British Prime Minister, gave command of the expedition against it to a young man of thirty-two, already distinguished in fighting in Europe and America. James Wolfe mustered his 9,000 men at Louisbourg, and in June of 1759 brought them up the St. Lawrence to the great French fortress, high on its cliffs. There he found himself faced by a much older French leader, the Marquis de Montcalm, who had indeed received a commission the year that Wolfe was born. The French forces were superior in numbers. For more than two months Montcalm, remaining on the defensive, baffled the besiegers. Finally, however, he was outwitted, and the British troops scaled the heights. The battle which followed, in which both commanders displayed exceptional gallantry and were mortally wounded, was one of the most memorable in modern history; and in Parkman's classic pages it has received a treatment worthy of the magnificent theme.*

FOR FULL two hours the procession of boats, borne on the current, steered silently down the St. Lawrence. The stars were visible, but the night was moonless and sufficiently dark. The General was in one of the foremost boats, and near him was a young midshipman, John Robinson, afterwards professor of natural philosophy in the University of Edinburgh. He used to tell in his later life how Wolfe, with a low voice, repeated Gray's "Elegy in a Country Churchyard" to the officers about him. Probably it was to relieve the intense strain of his thoughts. Among the rest was the verse which his own fate was soon to illustrate, "The paths of glory lead but to the grave."

"Gentlemen," he said, as his recital ended, "I would rather have written those lines than take Quebec." None were there to tell him that the hero is greater than the poet.

As they neared their destination, the tide bore them in towards the shore, and the mighty wall of rock and forest towered in darkness on their left. The dead stillness was suddenly broken by the sharp "*Qui vive!*" of a French sentry, invisible in the thick gloom. "*France!*" answered a Highland officer of Fraser's regiment from one of the boats of the light infantry. He had served in Holland, and spoke French fluently.

"*A quel régiment?*"

"*De la Reine,*" replied the Highlander. He knew that a part of that corps was with Bougainville. The sentry, expecting the convoy of provisions, was satisfied, and did not ask for the password.

Soon after, the foremost boats were passing the heights of Samos, when another sentry challenged them, and they could see him through the darkness running down to the edge of the water, within range of a pistolshot. In answer to his questions, the same officer replied, in French: "Provision boats. Don't make a noise; the English will hear us." In fact, the sloop of war *Hunter* was anchored in the stream not far off. This time, again, the sentry let them pass. In a few moments they rounded the headland above the Anse du Foulon. There was no sentry there. The strong current swept the boats of the light infantry a little below the intended landing place. They disembarked on a narrow strand at the foot of heights as steep as a hill covered with trees can be. The twenty-four volunteers led the way, climbing with what silence they might, closely followed by a much larger body. When they reached the top they saw in the dim light a cluster of tents at a short distance, and immediately made a dash at them. Vergor leaped from bed and tried to run off, but was shot in the heel and captured. His men, taken by surprise, made little resistance. One or two were caught, and the rest fled.

The main body of troops waited in their boats by the edge of the strand. The heights near by were cleft by a great ravine choked with forest trees, and in its depths ran a little brook called Ruisseau Saint-Denis, which, swollen by the late rains, fell plashing in the stillness over a rock. Other than this no sound could reach the strained ear of Wolfe but the gurgle of the tide and the cautious climbing of

his advance parties as they mounted the steeps at some little distance from where he sat listening. At length from the top came a
sound of musketshots, followed by loud huzzas, and he knew that
his men were masters of the position. The word was given; the
troops leaped from the boats and scaled the heights, some here,
some there, clutching at trees and bushes, their muskets slung at
their backs. Tradition still points out the place, near the mouth of
the ravine, where the foremost reached the top. Wolfe said to an
officer near him, "You can try it, but I don't think you'll get up."
He himself, however, found strength to drag himself up with the
rest. The narrow slanting path on the face of the heights had been
made impassable by trenches and abatis, but all obstructions were
soon cleared away, and then the ascent was easy. In the gray of the
morning the long file of red-coated soldiers moved quickly upward,
and formed in order on the plateau above. . . .

The day broke in clouds and threatening rain. Wolfe's battalions
were drawn up along the crest of the heights. No enemy was in sight,
though a body of Canadians had sallied from the town and moved
along the strand towards the landing place, whence they were quickly
driven back. He had achieved the most critical part of his enterprise;
yet the success that he coveted placed him in imminent danger. On
one side was the garrison of Quebec and the army of Beauport,
and Bougainville was on the other. Wolfe's alternative was victory
or ruin, for if he should be overwhelmed by a combined attack,
retreat would be hopeless. His feelings no man can know, but it
would be safe to say that hesitation or doubt had no part in them.

He went to reconnoiter the ground, and soon came to the Plains of
Abraham, so called from Abraham Martin, a pilot known as Maître
Abraham, who had owned a piece of land here in the early times
of the colony. The Plains were a tract of grass, tolerably level in
most parts, patched here and there with cornfields, studded with
clumps of bushes, and forming a part of the high plateau at the eastern end of which Quebec stood. On the south it was bounded by
the declivities along the St. Lawrence, on the north by those along
the St. Charles, or rather along the meadows through which that
lazy stream crawled like a writhing snake. At the place that Wolfe
chose for his battlefield the plateau was less than a mile wide.

Thither the troops advanced, marched by files till they reached the ground, and then wheeled to form their line of battle, which stretched across the plateau and faced the city. It consisted of six battalions and the detached grenadiers from Louisbourg, all drawn up in ranks three deep. Its right wing was near the brink of the heights along the St. Lawrence, but the left could not reach those along the St. Charles. On this side a wide space was perforce left open, and there was danger of being outflanked. To prevent this, Brigadier Townshend was stationed here with two battalions, drawn up at right angles with the rest, and fronting the St. Charles. The battalion of Webb's regiment, under Colonel Burton, formed the reserve; the third battalion of Royal Americans was left to guard the landing; and Howe's light infantry occupied a wood far in the rear. Wolfe, with Monckton and Murray, commanded the front line, on which the heavy fighting was to fall, and which, when all the troops had arrived, numbered less than thirty-five hundred men.

Quebec was not a mile distant, but they could not see it; for a ridge of broken ground intervened, called Buttes-à Neveu, about six hundred paces off. The first division of troops had scarcely come up when, about six o'clock, this ridge was suddenly thronged with white uniforms. It was the battalion of Guienne, arrived at the eleventh hour from its camp by the St. Charles. Some time after, there was hot firing in the rear. It came from a detachment of Bougainville's command attacking a house where some of the light infantry were posted. The assailants were repulsed, and the firing ceased. Light showers fell at intervals, besprinkling the troops as they stood patiently waiting the event.

Montcalm had passed a troubled night. Through all the evening the cannon bellowed from the ships of Saunders, and the boats of the fleet hovered in the dusk off the Beauport shore, threatening every moment to land. Troops lined the intrenchments till day, while the General walked the field that adjoined his headquarters till one in the morning, accompanied by the Chevalier Johnstone and Colonel Poulariez. Johnstone says that he was in great agitation, and took no rest all night. At daybreak he heard the sound of cannon above the town. It was the battery at Samos firing on the English ships. He had sent an officer to the quarters of Vaudreuil, which were much nearer Quebec, with orders to bring him word at once should anything unusual happen. But no word came, and about six o'clock he mounted and rode thither with Johnstone. As they advanced, the country behind the town opened more and more upon their sight; till at length, when opposite Vaudreuil's house, they saw across the St. Charles, some two miles away, the red ranks of British soldiers on the heights beyond.

"This is a serious business," Montcalm said, and sent off Johnstone at full gallop to bring up the troops from the center and left of the camp. Those of the right were in motion already, doubtless by the Governor's order. Vaudreuil came out of the house. Montcalm stopped for a few words with him; then set spurs to his horse, and rode over the bridge of the St. Charles to the scene of danger. He rode with a fixed look, uttering not a word.

The army followed in such order as it might, crossed the bridge in hot haste, passed under the northern rampart of Quebec, entered at the palace gate, and pressed on in headlong march along the quaint narrow streets of the warlike town: troops of Indians in scalp locks and war paint, a savage glitter in their deep-set eyes; bands of Canadians whose all was at stake — faith, country, and home; the colony regulars; the battalions of old France, a torrent of white uniforms and gleaming bayonets, La Sarre, Languedoc, Roussillon, Béarn — victors of Oswego, William Henry, and Ticonderoga. So they swept on, poured out upon the plain, some by the gate of St. Louis and some by that of St. John, and hurried, breathless, to where the banners of Guienne still fluttered on the ridge.

Montcalm was amazed at what he saw. He had expected a detachment, and he found an army. Full in sight before him stretched the lines of Wolfe: the close ranks of the English infantry, a silent wall of red, and the wild array of the Highlanders, with their waving tartans, and bagpipes screaming defiance. Vaudreuil had not come; but not the less was felt the evil of a divided authority and the jealousy of the rival chiefs. Montcalm waited long for the forces he had ordered to join him from the left wing of the army. He waited in vain. It is said that the Governor had detained them, lest the English should attack the Beauport shore. Even if they did so and succeeded, the French might defy them, could they but put Wolfe to rout on the Plains of Abraham. Neither did the garrison of Quebec come to the aid of Montcalm. He sent to Ramesay, its commander, for twenty-five fieldpieces which were on the palace battery. Ramesay would give him only three, saying that he wanted them for his own defense. There were orders and counterorders — misunderstanding, haste, delay, perplexity.

Montcalm and his chief officers held a council of war. It is said that he and they alike were for immediate attack. His enemies declare that he was afraid lest Vaudreuil should arrive and take command; but the Governor was not a man to assume responsibility at such a crisis. Others say that his impetuosity overcame his better judgment; and of this charge it is hard to acquit him. Bougainville was but a few miles distant, and some of his troops were much nearer; a messenger sent by way of Old Lorrette could have reached him in an hour and a half at most, and a combined attack in front and rear might have been concerted with him. If, moreover, Montcalm could have come to an understanding with Vaudreuil, his own force might have been strengthened by two or three thousand additional men from the town and the camp of Beauport; but he felt that there was no time to lose, for he imagined that Wolfe would soon be reinforced, which was impossible, and he believed that the English were fortifying themselves, which was no less an error. He has been blamed not only for fighting too soon, but for fighting at all. In this he could not choose. Fight he must, for Wolfe was now in a position to cut off all his supplies. His men were full of ardor, and he resolved to attack before their ardor cooled. He spoke a few words to them in his keen, vehement way. "I remember very well how he looked," one of the Canadians, then a boy of eighteen, used to say in his old age; "he rode a black or dark bay horse along the front of our lines, brandishing his sword, as if to excite us to do our duty. He wore a coat with wide sleeves, which fell back as he raised his arm, and showed the white linen of the wristband."

The English waited the result with a composure which, if not quite real, was at least well feigned. The three fieldpieces sent by Ramesay plied them with canister shot, and fifteen hundred Canadians and Indians fusilladed them in front and flank. Over all the plain, from behind bushes and knolls and the edge of cornfields, puffs of smoke sprang incessantly from the guns of these hidden marksmen. Skirmishers were thrown out before the lines to hold them in check, and the soldiers were ordered to lie on the grass to avoid the shot. The firing was liveliest on the English left, where bands of sharp-shooters got under the edge of the declivity, among thickets, and behind scattered houses, whence they killed and wounded a considerable number of Townshend's men. The light infantry were called up from the rear. The houses were taken and retaken, and one or more of them was burned.

Wolfe was everywhere. How cool he was, and why his followers loved him, is shown by an incident that happened in the course of the morning. One of his captains was shot through the lungs, and on recovering consciousness he saw the General standing at his side. Wolfe pressed his hand, told him not to despair, praised his services, promised him early promotion, and sent an aide-de-camp to Monckton to beg that officer to keep the promise if he himself should fall.

It was towards ten o'clock when, from the high ground on the right of the line, Wolfe saw that the crisis was near. The French on the ridge had formed themselves into three bodies, regulars in the center, regulars and Canadians on right and left. Two field-pieces, which had been dragged up the heights at Anse du Foulon, fired on them with grapeshot, and the troops, rising from the ground, prepared to receive them. In a few moments more they were in motion. They came on rapidly, uttering loud shouts, and firing as soon as they were within range. Their ranks, ill ordered at the best, were further confused by a number of Canadians who had been mixed among the regulars, and who, after hastily firing, threw themselves on the ground to reload. The British advanced a few rods, then halted and stood still. When the French were within forty paces, the word of command rang out, and a crash of musketry answered all along the line. The volley was delivered with remark-able precision. In the battalions of the center, which had suffered least from the enemy's bullets, the simultaneous explosion was afterwards said by French officers to have sounded like a cannon shot. Another volley followed, and then a furious clattering fire that lasted but a minute or two. When the smoke rose, a miserable sight was revealed: the ground cumbered with dead and wounded, the advancing masses stopped short and turned into a frantic mob, shouting, cursing, gesticulating. The order was given to charge.

Then over the field rose the British cheer, mixed with the fierce yell of the Highland slogan. Some of the corps pushed forward with the bayonet; some advanced firing. The clansmen drew their broadswords and dashed on, keen and swift as bloodhounds. At the English right, though the attacking column was broken to pieces, a fire was still kept up, chiefly, it seems, by sharpshooters from the bushes and cornfields, where they had lain for an hour or more. Here Wolfe himself led the charge, at the head of the Louisbourg grenadiers. A shot shattered his wrist. He wrapped his handkerchief about it and kept on. Another shot struck him, and he still advanced, when a third lodged in his breast. He staggered, and sat on the ground. Lieutenant Brown, of the grenadiers, one Henderson, a volunteer in the same company, and a private soldier, aided by an officer of artillery who ran to join them, carried him in their arms to the rear. He begged them to lay him down. They did so, and asked if he would have a surgeon. "There's no need," he answered; "it's all over with me." A moment after, one of them cried out, "They run; see how they run!" "Who run?" Wolfe demanded, like a man roused from sleep. "The enemy, sir. Egad, they give way everywhere!" "Go, one of you, to Colonel Burton," returned the dying man; "tell him to march Webb's regiment down to Charles River, to cut off their retreat from the bridge." Then, turning on his side, he murmured, "Now, God be praised, I will die in peace!" and in a few moments his gallant soul had fled.

Montcalm, still on horseback, was borne with the tide of fugitives towards the town. As he approached the walls a shot passed through his body. He kept his seat; two soldiers supported him, one on each side, and led his horse through the St. Louis gate. On the open space within, among the excited crowd, were several women, drawn, no doubt, by eagerness to know the result of the fight. One of them recognized him, saw the streaming blood, and shrieked, "*O mon Dieu! mon Dieu! le Marquis est tué!*" "It's nothing, it's nothing," replied the death-stricken man; "don't be troubled for me, my good friends."

Francis Parkman, Montcalm and Wolfe

# VI

## The Coming of the Revolution

*Charles Édouard Armand Dumaresq*

Signing the Declaration of Independence

# 25. Mohawks Spill Tea in Boston Harbor

*George III insisted upon a duty on tea imported by Americans. The revenue was trifling, but he regarded this tax as a matter of principle. When the colonists smuggled the commodity in from Holland, the king and his ministers took steps to cheapen English tea to such a level that Americans would find it lower priced, even with the duty added, than the smuggled substitute. They believed that the colonists would then buy. But the Americans were as firm upon a question of principle as the king. Popular wrath was aroused and committees representing Boston and five other towns resolved in November, 1773, to allow none of the tea to be landed. Under the leadership of Sam Adams Boston merchants and shopkeepers took matters into their own hands. Conservatives were scandalized by the destruction of property but John Adams wrote, "This is the most magnificent movement of all."*

THE TEA destroyed was contained in three ships, lying near each other, at what was called at that time Griffin's wharf, and were surrounded by armed ships of war; the commanders of which had publicly declared, that if the rebels, as they were pleased to style the Bostonians, should not withdraw their opposition to the landing of the tea before a certain day, the 17th day of December, 1773, they should on that day force it on shore, under the cover of their cannon's mouth. On the day preceding the seventeenth, there was a meeting of the citizens of the county of Suffolk, convened at one of the churches in Boston, for the purpose of consulting on what measures might be considered expedient to prevent the landing of the tea, or secure the people from the collection of the duty. At that meeting a committee was appointed to wait on Governor Hutchinson, and request him to inform them whether he would take any measures to satisfy the people on the object of the meeting. To the first application of this committee, the Governor told them he would give them a definite answer by five o'clock in the afternoon. At the hour appointed, the committee again repaired to the Governor's house, and on inquiry found he had gone to his country seat at Milton, a distance of about six miles. When the committee returned and informed the meeting of the absence of the Governor, there was a confused murmur among the members, and the meeting was immediately dissolved, many of them crying out, "Let every man do his duty, and be true to his country"; and there was a general huzza for Griffin's wharf. It was now evening, and I immediately dressed myself in the costume of an Indian, equipped with a small hatchet, which I and my associates denominated the tomahawk, with which, and a club, after having painted my face and hands with coal dust in the shop of a blacksmith, I repaired to Griffin's wharf, where the ships lay that contained the tea. When I first appeared in the street, after being thus disguised, I fell in with many who were dressed, equipped, and painted as I was, and who fell in with me, and marched in order to the place of our destination. When we arrived at the wharf, there were three of our number who assumed an authority to direct our operations, to which we readily submitted. They divided us into three parties, for the purpose of boarding the three ships which contained the tea at the same time. The name of him who commanded the division to which I was assigned was Leonard Pitt. The names of the other commanders I never knew. We were immediately ordered by the respective commanders to board all the ships at the same time, which we promptly obeyed. The commander of the division to which I belonged, as soon as we were on board the ship, appointed me boatswain, and ordered me to go to the captain and demand of him the keys to the hatches and a dozen candles. I made the demand accordingly, and the captain promptly replied, and delivered the articles; but requested me at the same time to do no damage to the ship or rigging. We then were ordered by our commander to open the hatches, and take out all the chests of tea

and throw them overboard, and we immediately proceeded to execute his orders; first cutting and splitting the chests with our
tomahawks, so as thoroughly to expose them to the effects of the
water. In about three hours from the time we went on board, we
had thus broken and thrown overboard every tea chest to be found
in the ship, while those in the other ships were disposing of the
tea in the same way, at the same time. We were surrounded by
British armed ships, but no attempt was made to resist us. We then
quietly retired to our several places of residence, without having
any conversation with each other, or taking any measures to discover who were our associates; nor do I recollect of our having had
the knowledge of the name of a single individual concerned in that
affair, except that of Leonard Pitt, the commander of my division,
whom I have mentioned. There appeared to be an understanding
that each individual should volunteer his services, keep his own
secret, and risk the consequences for himself. No disorder took
place during that transaction, and it was observed at that time,
that the stillest night ensued that Boston had enjoyed for many
months.

During the time we were throwing the tea overboard, there were
several attempts made by some of the citizens of Boston and its
vicinity to carry off small quantities of it for their family use. To
effect that object, they would watch their opportunity to snatch
up a handful from the deck, where it became plentifully scattered,
and put it into their pockets. One Captain O'Connor, whom I well
knew, came on board for that purpose, and when he supposed he
was not noticed, filled his pockets, and also the lining of his coat.
But I had detected him, and gave information to the captain of
what he was doing. We were ordered to take him into custody, and
just as he was stepping from the vessel, I seized him by the skirt
of his coat, and in attempting to pull him back, I tore it off; but
springing forward, by a rapid effort, he made his escape. He had,
however, to run a gauntlet through the crowd upon the wharf;
each one, as he passed, giving him a kick or a stroke.

Another attempt was made to save a little tea from the ruins of
the cargo by a tall, aged man who wore a large cocked hat and white
wig, which was fashionable at that time. He had slightly slipped
a little into his pocket, but being detected, they seized him, and tak-

ing his hat and wig from his head, threw them, together with the tea, of which they had emptied his pockets, into the water. In consideration of his advanced age, he was permitted to escape, with now and then a slight kick.

The next morning, after we had cleared the ships of the tea, it was discovered that very considerable quantities of it were floating upon the surface of the water; and to prevent the possibility of any of its being saved for use, a number of small boats were manned by sailors and citizens, who rowed them into those parts of the harbor wherever the tea was visible, and by beating it with oars and paddles, so thoroughly drenched it, as to render its entire destruction inevitable.

GEORGE HEWES, A Retrospect of the Boston Tea-Party

# 26. John Adams Journeys to the Continental Congress

*The punitive acts of Parliament against the province of Massachusetts which followed the destruction of the tea resulted in the adoption by the colonies of a plan for a general congress. Delegates were chosen by all the colonies except Georgia, and met in Philadelphia in September of 1774. John Adams, who had graduated from Harvard almost twenty years earlier, was one of the leading attorneys of Boston. He and Josiah Quincy, Jr., had defended the British soldiers arrested after the "Boston Massacre," obtaining the acquittal of all but two; and he had been prominent in the Massachusetts Legislature. A man of positive views, with a stiff, cold personality, and a rather suspicious temper, he took a radical attitude toward the issues between the colonies and the British government. His diary shows how little New Englanders were acquainted with New York and Pennsylvania, and how curious they were as to life therein.*

Boston. August 10, 1774. — Wednesday. The Committee for the Congress took their departure from Boston, from Mr. Cushing's house, and rode to Coolidge's, where they dined in company with a large number of gentlemen, who went out and prepared an entertainment for them at that place. A most kindly and affectionate meeting we had, and about four in the afternoon we took our leave of them, amidst the kind wishes and fervent prayers of every man in the company for our health and success. This scene was truly affecting, beyond all description affecting. I lodged at Colonel Buck's.

16. Tuesday. — At four we made for New Haven. Seven miles out of town, at a tavern, we met a great number of carriages and of horsemen who had come out to meet us. The sheriff of the county, and constable of the town, and the justices of peace, were in the train. As we were coming, we met others to the amount of I know not what number, but a very great one. As we came into the town, all the bells in town were set to ringing, and the people, men, women, and children, were crowding at the doors and windows as if it was to see a coronation. At nine o'clock the cannon were fired, about a dozen guns, I think.

These expressions of respect to us are intended as demonstrations of the sympathy of this people with the Massachusetts Bay and its capital, and to show their expectations from the Congress, and their determination to carry into execution whatever shall be agreed upon. No governor of a province nor general of an army was ever treated with so much ceremony and assiduity as we have been throughout the whole colony of Connecticut hitherto, but especially all the way from Hartford to New Haven inclusively.

20. Saturday. — We breakfasted at Day's, and arrived in the city of New York at ten o'clock, at Hull's, a tavern, the sign the Bunch of Grapes. We rode by several very elegant country seats before we came to the city. This city will be a subject of much speculation to me.

The streets of this town are vastly more regular and elegant than those of Boston, and the houses are more grand, as well as neat. They are almost all painted, brick buildings and all. In our walks they showed us the house of Mr. William Smith, one of their Council, and the famous lawyer, Mr. Thomas Smith, etc., Mr. Rivington's store, etc.

22. Monday. — This morning we took Mr. McDougall into our coach and rode three miles out of town to Mr. Morin Scott's to breakfast — a very pleasant ride. Mr. Scott has an elegant seat there, with Hudson's River just behind his house and a rural prospect all around him. Mr. Scott, his lady and daughter, and her husband, Mr. Litchfield, were dressed to receive us. We sat in a fine airy entry till called into a front room to breakfast. A more elegant breakfast I never saw — rich place, a very large silver coffeepot, a very large silver teapot, napkins of the very finest materials, toast, and bread, and butter in great perfection. After breakfast a plate of beautiful peaches, another of pears, and another of plums, and a muskmelon were placed on the table.

Mr. Scott, Mr. William Smith, and Mr. William Livingston are the triumvirate who figured away in younger life against the Church of England, who wrote the *Independent Reflector,* the *Watch Tower,* and other papers. They are all of them children of Yale College. Scott and Livingston are said to be lazy; Smith improves every moment of his time. Livingston is lately removed into New Jersey and is one of the delegates for that province.

23. Tuesday. — The way we have been in, of breakfasting, dining, drinking coffee, etc., about the city, is very disagreeable on some accounts. Although it introduces us to the acquaintance of many respectable people here, yet it hinders us from seeing the college, the churches, the printers' offices and booksellers' shops, and many other things which we should choose to see.

With all the opulence and splendor of this city, there is very little good breeding to be found. We have been treated with an assiduous respect, but I have not seen one real gentleman, one well-bred man, since I came to town. At their entertainments there is no conversation that is agreeable; there is no modesty, no attention to one another. They talk very loud, very fast, and all together. If they ask you a question, before you can utter three words of your answer, they will break out upon you again, and talk away.

29. Monday. — We crossed the ferry over Delaware River to the province of Pennsylvania. . . . After dinner we stopped at Frankfort, about five miles out of town. A number of carriages and

gentlemen came out of Philadelphia to meet us — Mr. Thomas Mifflin, Mr. McKean, of the lower counties, one of their delegates, Mr. Rutledge of Carolina, and a number of gentlemen from Philadelphia, Mr. Folsom and Mr. Sullivan, the New Hampshire delegates. We were introduced to all these gentlemen, and most cordially welcomed to Philadelphia. We then rode into town, and dirty, dusty, and fatigued as we were, we could not resist the importunity to go to the tavern, the most genteel one in America. Here we had a fresh welcome to the city of Philadelphia, and after some time spent in conversation, a curtain was drawn, and in the other half of the chamber a supper appeared as elegant as ever was laid upon a table. About eleven o'clock we retired.

31. Wednesday. — Made a visit to Governor Ward of Rhode Island at his lodgings. There we were introduced to several gentlemen. Mr. Dickinson, the farmer, of Pennsylvania, came in his coach with four beautiful horses to Mr. Ward's lodgings to see us. He was introduced to us, and very politely said he was exceedingly glad to have the pleasure of seeing these gentlemen; made some inquiry after the health of his brother and sister, who are now in Boston; gave us some account of his late ill health and his present gout. This was the first time of his getting out. Mr. Dickinson has been subject to hectic complaints. He is a shadow, tall, but slender as a reed, pale as ashes; one would think at first sight that he could not live a month, yet upon a more attentive inspection, he looks as if the springs of life were strong enough to last many years. We dined with Mr. Lynch, his lady and daughter, at their lodgings, Mrs. McKenzie's; and a very agreeable dinner and afternoon we had, notwithstanding the violent heat. We were all vastly pleased with Mr. Lynch. He is a solid, firm, judicious man. He told us that Colonel Washington made the most eloquent speech at the Virginia Convention that ever was made. Says he, "I will raise one thousand men, subsist them at my own expense, and march myself at their head for the relief of Boston."

The Diary of John Adams

# 27. "Give Me Liberty or Give Me Death!"

*Patrick Henry, prominent as a radical in opposing the measures of the British government, had sat in the First Continental Congress. As a member in 1775 of the revolutionary convention of Virginia, he believed war inevitable, and offered resolutions for arming the militia. Conservatives opposed this measure as premature. Henry then burst into this classic bit of eloquence. It was not written out or reported at the time, and the form undoubtedly owes something to Henry's biographer, William Wirt; but the substance and much of the phraseology is his own.*

MR. PRESIDENT: It is natural for man to indulge in the illusions of hope. We are apt to shut our eyes against a painful truth, and listen to the song of that siren till she transforms us into beasts. Is this the part of wise men, engaged in a great and arduous struggle for liberty? Are we disposed to be of the number of those who, having eyes, see not, and having ears, hear not, the things which so nearly concern their temporal salvation? For my part, whatever anguish of spirit it may cost, I am willing to know the whole truth; to know the worst, and to provide for it.

I have but one lamp by which my feet are guided, and that is the lamp of experience. I know of no way of judging of the future but by the past. And, judging by the past, I wish to know what there has been in the conduct of the British ministry for the last ten years to justify those hopes with which the gentlemen have been pleased to solace themselves and the House? Is it that insidious smile with which our petition has been lately received? Trust it not, sir; it will prove a snare to your feet. Suffer not yourselves to be betrayed with a kiss. Ask yourselves how this gracious reception of our petition comports with those warlike preparations which cover our waters and darken our land. Are fleets and armies necessary to a work of love and reconciliation? Have we shown ourselves so unwilling to be reconciled that force must be called in to win back our love? Let us not deceive ourselves, sir. These are the implements of war and subjugation, the last arguments to which kings resort.

I ask the gentlemen, sir, what means this martial array, if its purpose be not to force us to submission? Can the gentlemen assign any other possible motive for it? Has Great Britain any enemy in this quarter of the world, to call for all this accumulation of navies and armies? No, sir, she has none. They are meant for us; they can be meant for no other. They are sent over to bind and rivet upon us those chains which the British ministry have been so long forging. And what have we to oppose to them? Shall we try argument? Sir, we have been trying that for the last ten years. Have we anything new to offer upon the subject? Nothing. We have held the subject up in every light of which it is capable; but it has been all in vain.

Shall we resort to entreaty and humble supplication? What terms shall we find which have not been already exhausted? Let us not, I beseech you, sir, deceive ourselves longer. Sir, we have done everything that could be done, to avert the storm which is now coming on. We have petitioned, we have remonstrated, we have supplicated; we have prostrated ourselves before the throne, and have implored its interposition to arrest the tyrannical hands of the ministry and Parliament. Our petitions have been slighted; our remonstrances have produced additional violence and insult; our supplications have been disregarded; and we have been spurned, with contempt, from the foot of the throne. In vain, after these things, may we indulge the fond hope of peace and reconciliation. There is no longer any room for hope.

If we wish to be free; if we mean to preserve inviolate those inestimable privileges for which we have been so long contending; if we mean not basely to abandon the noble struggle in which we have been so long engaged, and which we have pledged ourselves never to abandon until the glorious object of our contest shall be obtained — we must fight! I repeat it, sir, we must fight! An appeal to arms, and to the God of hosts, is all that is left us.

They tell us, sir, that we are weak — unable to cope with so formidable an adversary. But when shall we be stronger? Will it be the next week or the next year? Will it be when we are totally disarmed, and when a British guard shall be stationed in every house? Shall we gather strength by irresolution and inaction? Shall we acquire the means of effectual resistance by lying supinely on our backs, and hugging the delusive phantom of hope, until our enemies shall have bound us hand and foot? Sir, we are not weak, if we make a proper use of those means which the God of nature hath placed in our power. Three millions of people, armed in the holy cause of Liberty, and in such a country as that which we possess, are invincible by any force which our enemy can send against us.

Besides, sir, we shall not fight our battles alone. There is a just God, who presides over the destinies of nations, and who will raise up friends to fight our battles for us. The battle, sir, is not to the strong alone; it is to the vigilant, the active, the brave. Besides, sir, we have no election. If we were base enough to desire it, it is now too late to retire from the contest. There is no retreat but in submission and slavery! Our chains are forged. Their clanking may be heard on the plains of Boston! The war is inevitable — and let it come! I repeat it, sir, let it come!

It is vain, sir, to extenuate the matter. The gentlemen may cry, Peace, peace! but there is no peace. The war has actually begun! The next gale that sweeps from the north will bring to our ears the clash of resounding arms! Our brethren are already in the field! Why stand we here idle? What is it that the gentlemen wish? What would they have? Is life so dear or peace so sweet as to be purchased at the price of chains and slavery? Forbid it, Almighty God. I know not what course others may take, but as for me, give me liberty or give me death!

WILLIAM WIRT, Life of Patrick Henry

# 28. Colonel Washington Scouts the Idea of Independence

*Jonathan Boucher, a conservative-minded clergyman of the Church of England in Maryland, undoubtedly gave a correct view of Washington's mind when he represented him, on his journey to the Second Continental Congress in 1775, as being still attached to Great Britain. Even after Lexington and Concord, most colonists hoped that with a redress of grievances the old relations with the crown could be restored; and Congress officially maintained this attitude long after it had sent Washington to take command at Cambridge.*

I HAPPENED to be going across the Potomac to Alexandria with my wife and some other of our friends exactly at the time that General Washington was crossing it on his way to the northward, whither he was going to take the command of the Continental Army. There had been a great meeting of people, and great doings, in Alexandria on the occasion; and everybody seemed to be on fire, either with rum or patriotism or both. Some patriots in our boat huzzaed, and gave three cheers to the General as he passed us; whilst Mr. Addison and myself contented ourselves with pulling off our hats. The General (then only Colonel) Washington beckoned us to stop, as we did, just, as he said, to shake us by the hand. His behavior to me was now, as it had always been, polite and respectful, and I shall forever remember what passed in the few disturbed moments of conversation we then had. From his going on the errand he was, I foresaw and apprized him of much that has since happened; in particular that there would certainly then be a civil war, and that the Americans would soon declare for independency. With more earnestness than was usual with his great reserve, he scouted my apprehensions, adding (and I believe with perfect sincerity) that if ever I heard of his joining in any such measures I had his leave to set him down for everything wicked. Like Hazael, he might have said, "Is thy servant a dog that he should do this great thing?" So little do men know of themselves, and so dangerous is it to make one false step. Many a man, it may be, has gone through life without ever making any egregiously false step; but I question if an instance can be named when a man having made one false step made but one. When once a man goes one mile from the strict line of rectitude, he soon sees, or fancies he sees, reasons compelling him to go *twain*. This was the last time I ever saw this gentleman, who, contrary to all reasonable expectation, has since so distinguished himself as that he will probably be handed down to posterity as one of the first characters of the age.

JONATHAN BOUCHER, Reminiscences of an American Loyalist

# 29. Adams Nominates Washington Commander-in-Chief

*John Adams, only less than his second cousin, Sam Adams, was from the beginning impatient for separation from England. He had great influence in the Continental Congress. Realizing that sectional harmony was indispensable, and that union of the colonies would be promoted if the commander of troops fighting on New England soil were a Virginian, he took the leading part in the presentation of Washington — whose superiority in experience over other aspirants was manifest — as commander-in-chief. This was in June, 1775, a full year before Adams seconded Richard Henry Lee's famous resolution that "these colonies are, and of right ought to be, free and independent States."*

IN SEVERAL conversations, I found more than one very cool about the appointment of Washington, and particularly Mr. Pendleton was very clear and full against it. Full of anxieties concerning these confusions, and apprehending daily that we should hear very distressing news from Boston, I walked with Mr. Samuel Adams in the State House yard, for a little exercise and fresh air, before the hour of Congress, and there represented to him the various dangers that surrounded us. He agreed to them all, but said, "What shall we do?" I answered him that he knew I had taken great pains to get our colleagues to agree upon some plan, that we might be unanimous; but he knew that they would pledge themselves to nothing; but I was determined to take a step which should compel them and all the other members of Congress to declare themselves for or against something. "I am determined this morning to make a direct motion that Congress should adopt the army before Boston, and appoint Colonel Washington commander of it." Mr. Adams seemed to think very seriously of it, but said nothing.

Accordingly, when Congress had assembled, I rose in my place, and in as short a speech as the subject would admit, represented the state of the Colonies, the uncertainty in the minds of the people, their great expectation and anxiety, the distresses of the army, the danger of its dissolution, the difficulty of collecting another, and the probability that the British army would take advantage of our delays, march out of Boston, and spread desolation as far as they could go. I concluded with a motion, in form, that Congress would adopt the army at Cambridge and appoint a general; that though this was not the proper time to nominate a general, yet, as I had reason to believe this was a point of the greatest difficulty, I had no hesitation to declare that I had but one gentleman in my mind for that important command, and that was a gentleman from Virginia who was among us and very well known to all of us, a gentleman whose skill and experience as an officer, whose independent fortune, great talents, and excellent universal character, would command the approbation of all America, and unite the cordial exertions of all the colonies better than any other person in the Union. Mr. Washington, who happened to sit near the door, as soon as he heard me allude to him, from his usual modesty, darted into the library room. Mr. Hancock — who was our president, which gave me an opportunity to observe his countenance while I was speaking on the state of the colonies, the army at Cambridge, and the enemy — heard me with visible pleasure; but when I came to describe Washington for the commander, I never remarked a more sudden and striking change of countenance. Mortification and resentment were expressed as forcibly as his face could exhibit them. Mr. Samuel Adams seconded the motion, and that did not soften the president's physiognomy at all. The subject came under debate, and several gentlemen declared themselves against the appointment of Mr. Washington, not on account of any personal objection against him, but because the army were all from New England, had a general of their own, appeared to be satisfied with him, and had proved themselves able to imprison the British army in Boston, which was all they expected or desired at that time. Mr. Pendleton, of Virginia, [and] Mr. Sherman, of Connecticut, were very explicit in declaring this opinion; Mr. Cushing and several others more faintly expressed their opposition, and their fears of discontents in the army and in New England. Mr. Paine expressed a great opinion of General Ward and a strong friendship for him, having been his classmate at college, or at least his contemporary; but gave no opinion upon the question. The subject was postponed to a future day. In the meantime, pains were taken out-of-doors to obtain a unanimity, and the voices were generally so clearly in favor of Washington, that the dissentient members were persuaded to withdraw their opposition, and Mr. Washington was nominated, I believe by Mr. Thomas Johnson of Maryland, unanimously elected, and the army adopted.

The Diary of John Adams

# 30. A Shot Is Fired That Is Heard around the World

*"What a glorious morning is this!"* exclaimed the exultant Sam Adams as he listened to the rattle of musketry on April 19, 1775. He realized that the events of that day made independence almost inevitable. Hostilities had almost begun in February, when General Thomas Gage sent a force by water to

*Salem to search for powder. On April 19th he hurried a force at dawn to Concord, twenty miles from Boston, to destroy the military stores which had been collected there. This narrative from a British pen places the blame for the first shots squarely on the colonists; but the latter had witnesses who declared that the British had fired first.*

O N THE evening of the 18th, about nine o'clock, I learned there was a large detachment going from this garrison, on which I immediately resolved to go with them, and meeting a few men in the street full accoutered, I followed them and embarked at the Magazine Guard and landed near Cambridge, where I joined Major Pitcairn, who I understood was to command next to Colonel Smith. Here we remained for two hours, partly waiting for the rest of the detachment and for provisions. About half an hour after two in the morning, on the 19th, we marched, Major Pitcairn commanding in front the light infantry. The tide being in, we were up to our middles before we got into the road. Continued for three miles without meeting with any person, when I heard Lieutenant Adair of the marines, who was a little before me in front, call out, "Here are two fellows galloping express to alarm the country," on which I immediately ran up to them, seized one of them and our guide the other, dismounted them, and by Major Pitcairn's directions, gave them in charge to the men. A little after, we were joined by Lieutenant Grant of the Royal Artillery, who told us the country, he was afraid, was alarmed, of which we had little reason to doubt as we heard several shots, being then between three and four in the morning (a very unusual time for firing), when we were joined by Major Mitchell, Captain Cochrane, Captain Lumm, and several other gentlemen who told us the whole country was alarmed and had galloped for their lives, or words to that purpose — that they had taken Paul [Revere], but were obliged to let him go after cutting his girths and stirrups. A little after, a fellow came out of a cross-road galloping. Mr. Adair and I called to him to stop, but he galloped off as hard as he could, upon which Mr. Simms, surgeon's mate of the Forty-Third Regiment, who was on horseback, pursued him and took him a great way in front. A little after, I met a very genteel man riding in a carriage they call a sulky, who assured me there were six hundred men assembled at Lexington with a view of opposing us. I think I should know the man again if I saw him, as I took very particular notice of his features and dress. I waited with him till Major Pitcairn came up with the division, to whom he repeated much the same as he did to me. Then going on in front again, I met, coming out of a crossroad, another fellow galloping. However, hearing him some time before, I placed myself so that I got hold of the bridle of his horse and dismounted him. Our guide seemed to think that this was a very material fellow and said something as if he had been a member of the provincial Congress. A little after this I mounted a horse I had, and Mr. Adair went into a chaise. It began now to be daylight and we met some men with a wagon of wood, who told us there were odds of a thousand men in arms at Lexington and added that they would fight us. Here we waited for some time, but seeing nothing of the divisions, I rode to the left about half a mile to see if I could fall in with them, but could see nothing of them. However, saw a vast number of the country militia going over the hill with their arms, to Lexington, and met one of them in the teeth whom I obliged to give up his firelock and bayonet, which I believe he would not have done so easily but from Mr. Adair's coming up. On this, we turned back the road we came and found the division who had halted in consequence of the intelligence the man in the sulky gave them, in order to make a disposition, by advancing men in front and on the flanks, to prevent a surprise. I went on with the front party, which consisted of a sergeant and six or eight men. I shall observe here that the road before you go into Lexington is level for about a thousand yards. Here we saw shots fired to the right and left of us, but as we heard no whizzing of balls, I conclude they were to alarm the body that was there of our approach. On coming within gunshot of the village of Lexington, a fellow from the corner of the road, on the right hand, cocked his piece at me, burnt priming [flashed in the pan]. I immediately called to Mr. Adair and the party to observe this circumstance, which they did, and I acquainted Major Pitcairn of it immediately.

We still went on farther when three shot more were fired at us, which we did not return, and this is sacred truth as I hope for mercy.

These three shot were fired from a corner of a large house to the right of the church. When we came up to the main body, which appeared to me to exceed four hundred in and about the village, who were drawn up in a plain opposite to the church, several officers called out, "Throw down your arms and you shall come to no harm," or words to that effect. Which, they refusing to do, instantaneously the gentlemen who were on horseback rode in amongst them, of which I was one, at which instant I heard Major Pitcairn's voice call out, "Soldiers, don't fire; keep your ranks; form and surround them." Instantly some of the villains, who got over the hedge, fired at us, which our men for the first time returned, which set my horse a-going, who galloped with me down a road above six hundred yards among the middle of them before I turned him. And in returning, a vast number who were in a wood at the right of the grenadiers fired at me, but the distance was so great that I only heard the whistling of the balls, but saw a great number of people in the wood. In consequence of their discovering themselves by firing, our grenadiers gave them a smart fire.

William Sutherland's Letter April 27, 1775

# 31. Jefferson Writes the Declaration of Independence

*Although Jefferson can be said never to have made a real speech, he held a pen which gave him an enormous influence from young manhood to old age. He wrote elaborate resolutions for the first revolutionary convention of Virginia in 1774, later publishing them as a pamphlet under the title* A Summary View of the Rights of America. *This work, of which numerous editions were printed in England, gave Jefferson a place among the most influential of American leaders. A little later he drafted Virginia's reply to the conciliatory proposals of Lord North, and followed this by writing the reply of Congress to the same proffer. The fame won by these documents pointed him out as the logical man to draft an explanation and defense of the action of the colonies in separating from England. As John Adams says, most of the ideas were old. In fact, some of the most essential were drawn from the writings of John Locke. But the immortal phraseology of the preamble was strictly Jefferson's.*

YOU INQUIRE why so young a man as Mr. Jefferson was placed at the head of the committee for preparing a Declaration of Independence? I answer: It was the Frankfort advice, to place Virginia at the head of everything. Mr. Richard Henry Lee might be gone to Virginia, to his sick family, for aught I know, but that was not the reason of Mr. Jefferson's appointment. There were three committees appointed at the same time, one for the Declaration of Independence, another for preparing articles of confederation, and another for preparing a treaty to be proposed to France. Mr. Lee was chosen for the Committee of Confederation, and it was not thought convenient that the same person should be upon both. Mr. Jefferson came into Congress in June, 1775, and brought with him a reputation for literature, science, and a happy talent of composition. Writings of his were handed about, remarkable for the peculiar felicity of expression. Though a silent member in Congress, he was so prompt, frank, explicit, and decisive upon committees and in conversation — not even Samuel Adams was more so — that he soon seized upon my heart; and upon this occasion I gave him my vote, and did all in my power to procure the votes of others. I think he had one more vote than any other, and that placed him at the head of the committee. I had the next highest number, and that placed me the second. The committee met, discussed the subject, and then appointed Mr. Jefferson and me to make the draft, I suppose because we were the two first on the list.

The subcommittee met. Jefferson proposed to me to make the draft. I said, "I will not." "You should do it." "Oh! no." "Why will you not? You ought to do it." "I will not." "Why?" "Reasons enough." "What can be your reasons?" "Reason first, you are a Virginian, and a Virginian ought to appear at the head of this business. Reason second, I am obnoxious, suspected, and unpopular. You are very much otherwise. Reason third, you can write ten times better than I can." "Well," said Jefferson, "if you are decided, I will do as well as I can." "Very well. When you have drawn it up, we will have a meeting."

A meeting we accordingly had, and conned the paper over. I was delighted with its high tone and the flights of oratory with which it abounded, especially that concerning Negro slavery, which, though I knew his Southern brethren would never suffer to pass in Congress, I certainly never would oppose. There were other expressions which I would not have inserted if I had drawn it up, particularly that which called the King tyrant. I thought this too personal, for I never believed George to be a tyrant in disposition and in nature; I always believed him to be deceived by his courtiers on both sides of the Atlantic, and in his official capacity, only, cruel. I thought the expression too passionate, and too much like scolding, for so grave and solemn a document; but as Franklin and Sherman were to inspect it afterwards, I thought it would not become me to strike it out. I consented to report it, and do not now remember that I made or suggested a single alteration.

We reported it to the committee of five. It was read, and I do not remember that Franklin or Sherman criticized anything. We were all in haste. Congress was impatient, and the instrument was reported, as I believe, in Jefferson's handwriting, as he first drew it. Congress cut off about a quarter of it, as I expected they would; but they obliterated some of the best of it, and left all that was exceptionable, if anything in it was. I have long wondered that the original draft had not been published. I suppose the reason is the vehement philippic against Negro slavery.

As you justly observe, there is not an idea in it but what had been hackneyed in Congress for two years before. The substance of it is contained in the declaration of rights and the violation of those rights in the Journals of Congress in 1774. Indeed, the essence of it is contained in a pamphlet, voted and printed by the town of Boston, before the first Congress met, composed by James Otis, as I suppose, in one of his lucid intervals, and pruned and polished by Samuel Adams.

JOHN ADAMS, Letter to Timothy Pickering, August 6, 1822

# 32. The United States Declare Independence

*The best-known of American state papers, Jefferson's Declaration of Independence, is next to Lincoln's Second Inaugural Address also the noblest. It is of course the generalizations which give it nobility. Most of the specific statements on American grievances are decidedly partisan; some of them are historically open to controversy — even to grave question. But its statements upon the rights of man and the rights of Americans have inherent dignity, elevation, and truth. We may admit that Adams was right when he said that the general arguments of the Declaration were not fresh, and even that Rufus Choate spoke with some justice when he asserted that the paper was full of "glittering and high-sounding generalities." Asserting great basic truths, it was not intended to seek out novel ideas. But it set forth these truths with the logical force of John Locke, with a measured eloquence characteristic of the eighteenth century, and with a fervent idealism that was all Jefferson's own. Some of the phrases have been watchwords of democracy ever since.*

*In Congress, July 4, 1776,*

The unanimous Declaration of the thirteen united States of America,

When in the Course of human events, it becomes necessary for one people to dissolve the political bands which have connected them with another, and to assume among the Powers of the earth, the separate and equal station to which the Laws of Nature and of Nature's God entitle them, a decent respect to the opinions of mankind requires that they should declare the causes which impel them to the separation.

We hold these truths to be self-evident, that all men are created equal, that they are endowed by their Creator with certain unalienable Rights, that among these are Life, Liberty and the pursuit of Happiness. That to secure these rights, Governments are instituted among Men, deriving their just powers from the consent of the governed. That whenever any Form of Government becomes destructive of these ends, it is the Right of the People to alter or to abolish it, and to institute new Government, laying its foundation on such principles and organizing its powers in such form, as to them shall seem most likely to effect their Safety and Happiness. Prudence, indeed, will dictate that Governments long established should not be changed for light and transient causes; and accordingly all experience hath shown, that mankind are more disposed to suffer, while evils are sufferable, than to right themselves by abolishing the forms to which they are accustomed. But when a long train of abuses and usurpations, pursuing invariably the same Object evinces a design to reduce them under absolute Despotism, it is their right, it is their duty, to throw off such Government, and to provide new Guards for their future security. — Such has been the patient sufferance of these Colonies; and such is now the necessity which constrains them to alter their former Systems of Government. The history of the present King of Great Britain is a history of repeated injuries and usurpations, all having in direct object the establishment of an absolute Tyranny over these States. To prove this, let Facts be submitted to a candid world.

He has refused his Assent to Laws, the most wholesome and necessary for the public good.

He has forbidden his Governors to pass Laws of immediate and pressing importance, unless suspended in their operation till his Assent should be obtained; and when so suspended, he has utterly neglected to attend to them.

He has refused to pass other Laws for the accommodation of large districts of people, unless those people would relinquish the right of Representation in the Legislature, a right inestimable to them and formidable to tyrants only.

He has called together legislative bodies at places unusual, uncomfortable, and distant from the depository of their Public Records, for the sole purpose of fatiguing them into compliance with his measures.

He has dissolved Representative Houses repeatedly, for opposing with manly firmness his invasions on the rights of the people.

He has refused for a long time, after such dissolutions, to cause others to be elected; whereby the Legislative Powers, incapable of Annihilation, have returned to the People at large for their exercise; the State remaining in the mean time exposed to all the dangers of invasion from without, and convulsions within.

He has endeavoured to prevent the population of these States; for that purpose obstructing the Laws of Naturalization of Foreigners; refusing to pass others to encourage their migration hither, and raising the conditions of new Appropriations of Lands.

He has obstructed the Administration of Justice, by refusing his Assent to Laws for establishing Judiciary Powers.

He has made Judges dependent on his Will alone, for the tenure of their offices, and the amount and payment of their salaries.

He has erected a multitude of New Offices, and sent hither swarms of Officers to harass our People, and eat out their substance.

He has kept among us, in times of peace, Standing Armies without the Consent of our legislature.

He has affected to render the Military independent of and superior to the Civil Power.

He has combined with others to subject us to a jurisdiction foreign to our constitution, and unacknowledged by our laws; giving his Assent to their acts of pretended legislation:

For quartering large bodies of armed troops among us:

For protecting them, by a mock Trial, from Punishment for any Murders which they should commit on the Inhabitants of these States:

For cutting off our Trade with all parts of the world:

For imposing taxes on us without our Consent:

For depriving us in many cases, of the benefits of Trial by Jury:

For transporting us beyond Seas to be tried for pretended offences:

For abolishing the free System of English Laws in a neighbouring Province, establishing therein an Arbitrary government, and enlarging its Boundaries so as to render it at once an example and fit instrument for introducing the same absolute rule into these Colonies:

For taking away our Charters, abolishing our most valuable Laws, and altering fundamentally the Forms of our Governments:

For suspending our own Legislature, and declaring themselves invested with Power to legislate for us in all cases whatsoever.

He has abdicated Government here, by declaring us out of his Protection and waging War against us.

He has plundered our seas, ravaged our Coasts, burnt our towns, and destroyed the lives of our people.

He is at this time transporting large armies of foreign mercenaries to compleat the works of death, desolation and tyranny, already begun with circumstances of Cruelty & perfidy scarcely paralleled in the most barbarous ages, and totally unworthy the Head of a civilized nation.

He has constrained our fellow Citizens taken Captive on the high Seas to bear Arms against their Country, to become the executioners of their friends and Brethren, or to fall themselves by their Hands.

He has excited domestic insurrections amongst us, and has endeavoured to bring on the inhabitants of our frontiers, the merciless Indian Savages, whose known rule of warfare, is an undistinguished destruction of all ages, sexes and conditions.

In every stage of these Oppressions We have Petitioned for Redress in the most humble terms: Our repeated Petitions have been answered only by repeated injury. A Prince, whose character is thus marked by every act which may define a Tyrant, is unfit to be the ruler of a free People.

Nor have We been wanting in attention to our British brethren. We have warned them from time to time of attempts by their legislature to extend an unwarrantable jurisdiction over us. We have reminded them of the circumstances of our emigration and settlement here. We have appealed to their native justice and magnanimity, and we have conjured them by the ties of our common kindred to disavow these usurpations, which would inevitably interrupt our connections and correspondence. They too have been deaf to the voice of justice and of consanguinity. We must, therefore, acquiesce in the necessity, which denounces our Separation, and hold them, as we hold the rest of mankind, Enemies in War, in Peace Friends.

We, therefore, the Representatives of the united States of America, in General Congress, Assembled, appealing to the Supreme Judge of the world for the rectitude of our intentions, do, in the Name, and by Authority of the good People of these Colonies, solemnly publish and declare, That these United Colonies are, and of Right ought to be Free and Independent States; that they are Absolved from all Allegiance to the British Crown, and that all political connection between them and the State of Great Britain, is and ought to be totally dissolved; and that as Free and Independent States, they have full Power to levy War, conclude Peace, contract Alliances, establish Commerce, and to do all other Acts and Things which Independent States may of right do. And for the support of this Declaration, with a firm reliance on the Protection of Divine Providence, we mutually pledge to each other our Lives, our Fortunes and our sacred Honor.

# VII

## The Winning of Independence

General von Steuben Drilling Troops at Valley Forge

# 33. Ethan Allen Captures Fort Ticonderoga

*The embattled colonists needed cannon and stores; also they wished to seize the gateway to Canada. To encompass these two objects, hardy fighters from Connecticut, Massachusetts, and what shortly became Vermont joined in a spring march on Ticonderoga, key fortress of northern New York. Their leader was the Vermonter Ethan Allen, who tells the story spiritedly.*

EVER since I arrived at the state of manhood, and acquainted myself with the general history of mankind, I have felt a sincere passion for liberty. The history of nations doomed to perpetual slavery in consequence of yielding up to tyrants their natural-born liberties, I read with a sort of philosophical horror; so that the first systematical and bloody attempt, at Lexington, to enslave America, thoroughly electrified my mind, and fully determined me to take part with my country. And, while I was wishing for an opportunity to signalize myself in its behalf, directions were privately sent to me from the then colony (now State) of Connecticut, to raise the Green Mountain Boys, and, if possible, with them to surprise and take the fortress of Ticonderoga. This enterprise I cheerfully undertook; and, after first guarding all the several passes that led thither, to cut off all intelligence between the garrison and the country, made a forced march from Bennington, and arrived at the lake opposite to Ticonderoga, on the evening of the 9th day of May, 1775, with two hundred and thirty valiant Green Mountain Boys; and it was with the utmost difficulty that I procured boats to cross the lake. However, I landed eighty-three men near the garrison, and sent the boats back for the rear guard, commanded by Colonel Seth Warner; but the day began to dawn, and I found myself under the necessity to attack the fort, before the rear could cross the lake; and, as it was viewed hazardous, I harangued the officers and soldiers in the manner following:

"Friends and fellow soldiers, you have, for a number of years past, been a scourge and terror to arbitrary power. Your valor has been famed abroad, and acknowledged, as appears by the advice and orders to me, from the General Assembly of Connecticut, to surprise and take the garrison now before us. I now propose to advance before you, and, in person, conduct you through the wicket gate; for we must this morning either quit our pretensions to valor, or possess ourselves of this fortress in a few minutes; and, inasmuch as it is a desperate attempt, which none but the bravest of men dare undertake, I do not urge it on any contrary to his will. You that will undertake voluntarily, poise your firelocks."

The men being, at this time, drawn up in three ranks, each poised his firelock. I ordered them to face to the right, and, at the head of the center file, marched them immediately to the wicket gate aforesaid, where I found a sentry posted, who instantly snapped his fusee at me; I ran immediately toward him, and he retreated through the covered way into the parade within the garrison, gave a halloo, and ran under a bombproof. My party, who followed me into the fort, I formed on the parade in such a manner as to face the two barracks which faced each other.

The garrison being asleep, except the sentries, we gave three huzzas, which greatly surprised them. One of the sentries made a pass at one of my officers with a charged bayonet, and slightly wounded him. My first thought was to kill him with my sword; but, in an instant, I altered the design and fury of the blow to a slight cut on the side of the head, upon which he dropped his gun, and asked quarter, which I readily granted him, and demanded of him the place where the commanding officer kept; he showed me a pair of stairs in the front of a barrack, on the west part of the garrison, which led up to a second story in said barrack, to which I immediately repaired, and ordered the commander, Captain de la Place, to come forth instantly, or I would sacrifice the whole garrison; at which the Captain came immediately to the door, with his breeches in his hand, when I ordered him to deliver me the fort instantly; he asked me by what authority I demanded it: I answered him, "*In the name of the great Jehovah and the Continental Congress.*" The authority of the Congress being very little known at that time, he began to speak again; but I interrupted him, and with my drawn sword over his head, again demanded an immediate surrender of the garrison; with which he then complied, and ordered his men to be forthwith paraded without arms, as he had given up the garrison. In the meantime some of my officers had given orders, and in consequence thereof, sundry of the barrack doors were beat down, and about one-third of the garrison imprisoned, which consisted of the said commander, a Lieutenant Feltham, a conductor of artillery, a gunner, two sergeants, and forty-four rank and file; about one hundred pieces of cannon, one thirteen-inch mortar, and a number of swivels. This surprise was carried into execution in the gray of the morning of the 10th of May, 1775. The sun seemed to rise that morning with a superior luster, and Ticonderoga and its dependencies smiled to its conquerors, who tossed about the flowing bowl, and wished success to Congress, and the liberty and freedom of America.

ETHAN ALLEN, Narrative of Captivity

# 34. William Humphrey Marches with Arnold to Quebec

*Among the immortal marches of American forces against distant objectives — Benedict Arnold's march upon Quebec, George Rogers Clark's march upon Fort Kaskaskia, Frémont's march with the California Battalion upon Los Angeles — the first-named combines tragedy with heroism in an unforgettable way. Young Benedict Arnold, who had led a militia company from New Haven to Cambridge, and who had raised additional troops for the expedition against Ticonderoga, in which he reluctantly yielded first place to Ethan Allen, was ordered in the summer of 1775 to co-operate with General Richard Montgomery in an invasion of Canada.*

*He led his force of eleven hundred men out of Cambridge on September 17, 1775, and was soon advancing through the morasses and tangled woods of the Maine wilderness. Terrible hardships from cold, hunger, and disease killed many of his men and caused others to desert. When he reached Quebec winter was at hand, and the combined attack which he and Montgomery delivered on the last day of 1775 was a dismal failure.*

OCTOBER 16, 1775. — This day, being very short of provisions and brought to one half-pint of flour per man, and waiting until nine o'clock for the rifle companies, in order to get some supplies, they not coming up, we proceeded on our way. Came to an Indian hut, where one Sabatis lived, as big a rogue as ever existed under heaven; still proceeded on our way, marched about four miles and encamped, and Colonel Arnold came up in the evening at about eight o'clock, and hearing of our want of bread, ordered four bateaux with thirty-two men of each division to return to the rear for a supply of provision in the morning.

Here our company had not five or six pounds of flour to fifty men. I was sent back with this detachment with a great deal of reluctance.

October 20. — This day it rained very hard — our boats not having got up, we packed up our cartridges in casks in order to be ready for an immediate embarkation here. Stayed this night, it being the third day that we have been obliged to lay by for a supply of provision.

October 21. — This day it rained very hard and was almost as heavy a storm as I ever was sensible of. Colonel Enos came up with us at about eleven o'clock, and expected to have found Colonel Arnold, but on his not finding him, returned back, drove up his rear in the afternoon. Major Bigelow, who had been down with our boats for provision, returned, with only two barrels of flour. We are very short of provisions, and there is no probability of getting any more until we get to Sertigan. Now we have no other view than either to proceed to Canada or to retreat. We concluded to send all those back who were not able to do actual duty. This night the river rose to a high degree, better than two feet and a half, which occasions the current to run very swift. Our encampment grew very uncomfortable, especially for those who had no tents, and not being used to soldiers' fare.

October 25.— We are absolutely in a dangerous situation; however, I hope for the best, but if we receive no supplies from the French side, we shall be poorly off.

This day there [were] a subaltern and forty-eight men of the sick went back with three bateaux. The river is narrow and exceeding swift, the going by land is very bad, the men are very much disheartened and desirous to return; however, if their bellies were full, I believe they would rather go forward — we are out and must go on. Colonel Arnold has sent Captain Hanchet with a party to purchase of the French if possible, and to clear the roads. Here a council of war determined that Colonel Enos should not go back.

October 28.— At four o'clock an express came from Colonel Arnold, with intelligence that the French [were] glad to receive us, and that they would supply us with provision — glad tidings to people that are brought to one half-pint of flour, and but very little meat. Today was delivered out all the meat we had in our battalion, which turned out two ounces of meat per man. An express passed us to go to his Excellency General Washington; a pilot was sent us to lead us the right way through the woods; two companies of the musketry are gone forward, but the three rifle companies stayed with us; this is the nineteenth carrying place.

October 30.— This day we proceeded through a swamp six miles and more in frozen water and mud half-leg-high — got into an alder swamp; steering east-southerly came to a small river which we forded; the water was middle-high and very cold. This river is about eight rods wide. From thence we proceeded to a hill and there shaped our course to another river that we crossed on a log — here several of our men had the luck to fall in. I must confess that I began to be concerned about our situation, having only four days' provision in this wilderness where there was no sign of any human being, but a swampy thicket of wood made only for an asylum of wild beasts.

November 1.— This day we proceeded on our way — our people grew very much fatigued and began to fall in the rear, being very much reduced with hunger and cold. I saw, with astonishment, a dog killed and even eat, his paunch, guts, and skin. Went about twelve miles and encamped.

November 2. — This day we proceeded on our way through much fatigue, sixteen miles. It is an astonishing thing to see every man without any sustenance but cold water — this, you must think, is weakening rather than strengthening. — Here a boy returns and tells us that there was provision within eight miles of us. I saw several, when they came to see the provision, shed tears, they were so much overjoyed at the sight of relief.

November 3. — This day we proceeded on our way and met the provision, got refreshed, then set out again; passed by a pair of falls and went one mile and encamped.

November 9. — This day proceeded six miles through settlements, then entered the woods, which is nine miles, went fifteen miles and stayed at St. Mary's parish at a house near the chapel of the same name; there dined, and set out again to Point Levy, where we arrived at eight o'clock. Found Colonel Arnold and our volunteers all well and in good spirits.

December 27. — This day stormy — the men were ordered to hold themselves in readiness to the shortest notice at about twelve at night, the army being divided according to the plan the General had laid. Part of our detachment proceeded to the hill, the other part stayed to attack the lower town under the command of Colonel Arnold; but, it clearing up, it was thought prudent to defer storming the garrison until a favorable opportunity.

December 28. — This day some of our men took four men that refused to turn out, and led them round with halters round their necks, from place to place, and treated them in such a manner as all such villains deserve. The General issued an order to the satisfaction of the soldiers in general, of the pleasure that he took in seeing the men so expert and alert in turning out in order to storm the city of Quebec.

December 30. — This day the enemy kept up a smart fire all day upon St. Roche's, but did little or no damage. This evening about ten o'clock, received orders that it was the General's determination to storm the city of Quebec; then we ordered our men to get their arms in readiness for to go and storm. It was very dark and snowed. The plan for executing the design is as follows: General Montgomery with the York troops to proceed round Cape Diamond to a place by the name of "The Potash" and make their attack there. Colonel Livingston, with a party of Canadians, to make a false attack upon Cape Diamond and St. John's Gate. An advance party of twenty-five men to proceed to D—— wharf. Colonel Arnold's detachment to attack the lower town. We were to receive a signal by three sky-rockets when to attack — but, not observing them, we was about half an hour too late. Captain Dearborn's company on account of being quartered on the other side of the Charles River, and the tide being high, not coming up, we proceeding without them, expecting them to drive up the rear, we forced and took the guard. Captain was drunk and not able to stand on his legs without assistance. . . . They fired very briskly upon us; we passed along the street, and they killed and wounded a number of our men. After we had gained the first barricade, we halted our men and tried to scale the second barrier — and, notwithstanding their utmost efforts, we got some of our ladders up and were obliged to retreat, our guns being wet, as not one in ten would fire. Then we concluded to retreat, which we did to first barrier that we had took, and when we came there, we found we could not retreat without losing all our men, or at least the most of them. There was killed of our party Lieutenant Humphrey and Lieutenant Cooper, together with Captain Hendricks, with a number of privates. And in General Montgomery's party there was killed the brave General Montgomery, his aide-de-camp Macpherson, Captain Cheesman, and some privates.

Colonel Campbell then took command and ordered them to retreat, so that the force of the garrison came upon us. Captain Lamb, among the rest, was wounded. There was no possibility of our retreating; they promising us good quarter, we surrendered ourselves. Colonel Arnold, being wounded in the front of the action, was carried off to the general hospital. Thus after a long and tedious march I have been unfortunate enough to become a prisoner.

WILLIAM HUMPHREY, Journal

# 35. Shaw Deplores Conditions in the American Army

*Until almost the close of the year 1776 the war seemed to be, from the patriot point of view, a dismal failure. Washington lost the battle of Long Island, and was lucky to evacuate his army before it was captured by the British. His attempt to hold New York city failed, and Howe's capture of Fort Washington at the upper end of Manhattan Island compelled a further retreat. It is not strange that the morale of the American forces sank to a low ebb. From their discouragement, however, Washington's brilliant little victories over British outposts at Trenton and Princeton soon rescued them.*

OCTOBER 11, 1776 [Fort Washington, New York].— The army still remain in tents. It will be late in the season before we get into huts or barracks. After our retreat from the city, our troops had a skirmish with the enemy and repulsed them. Though in itself it was a small affair, the consequences were great, as the check they received will probably be a means of keeping off an attack till the spring. This is devoutly to be wished, for the aspect of our affairs at present is not very flattering, I assure you. However, we hope soon to be in a very fine way, as the Congress, *at last,* seem to think the war must be carried on upon a large scale; eighty-eight battalions of seven hundred and odd men each, besides a proportionable number of artillery, with everything necessary to such an army as we must have, are to be raised. No more militia are to be called in; and, in my humble opinion, they are productive of more expense than the keeping an equal or larger number of regular troops, to say nothing of the little service they have been to us anywhere but in New England. Those from the Jerseys, and other places this way, on the appearance of the enemy, scampered off by whole companies and regiments, especially when the enemy's ships came before a fort of ours at Paulus

Hook, opposite the city of New York, about a mile and a quarter distant. So great a panic seized them that Captain Dana of our regiment was obliged to charge his cannon with grapeshot and threaten to fire on them; otherwise they would have abandoned the place before he could get the military stores off. These were your Southern heroes, fellows who affect to hold the Eastern Yankees in contempt; but I challenge them to produce an instance of cowardice in our people anyway equal to this of theirs. But I don't mean to enlarge on so ungrateful a subject. Comparisons are odious. There are, without doubt, good men among them; and it would be well if every distinction of this or that colony or province could be buried in that of *American*. I wish we had more Boston young fellows among us, for I think it rather disgraceful for so many of them to be idling at home these stirring times; and if they don't turn out, they will, when the war is over, appear very contemptible. . . .

November 18, 1776. — As for our army, God help it! — for at present it is in a disagreeable state; the militia gone and going home, the time of enlistment for our regular troops expiring, and little or nothing done towards raising new ones. The severities of the present campaign will discourage many from engaging again without large bounties, so that I do not think it improbable some of the states will be under a necessity of drafting men during the war. Very different this from the last, when many, without doubt, entered into the service merely for amusement. Ever since we left New England, we have been carrying on the war in an enemy's country, and firmly I believe, if Heaven had not something very great in store for America, we should ere this have been a ruined people. When I left the town of Boston with a view of joining our army, my enthusiasm was such as to induce me to think I should find as much public virtue among our people as is recorded of ancient Sparta or Rome. Numberless instances might be brought to show how miserably I was disappointed. Let it suffice to mention one. The militia whose times expired yesterday were desired to tarry for the good of their country *only four days,* and out of their whole number there were not sufficient to form one regiment who would engage. Scandalous! Tell it not in Britain. I cannot wish them a severer punishment than a due reward of their ingratitude. After the new army is raised, which must be done by some means or other, I hope we shall never be again so grossly infatuated as to expect any good can accrue from calling in the militia. Far be it from me to reflect on them as individuals. I speak of them as a body, which from its present constitution can be of no service to us; for, so long as men are under no obligation to stay after a limited time, at the expiration of which neither a regard for the welfare of their country nor a concern for their own honor can prevail on them, they must be not only ungrateful, but a dangerous part of society. You may perhaps, before this reaches you, be informed of Fort Washington's being in the hands of the enemy. They got possession of it the day before yesterday. We have not yet learnt the particulars, only that they made a feint of attacking some lines of ours below the fort, which induced the commanding officer to send a part of his force there. This the enemy took advantage of, by marching a number of troops they had previously prepared for the purpose between them and the fort, which, cutting off the communication, obliged them first — and shortly after, the fort, — to surrender, on what terms is not known. I was at General Lee's just after the news came. He was in a towering passion, and said that it was a splendid affair for Mr. Howe, who was returning chagrined and disgraced at being able to make no further progress this campaign, thus *to have his sores licked by us*. However, don't let us be discouraged, for we must expect greater rubs before an empire can be established.

The Journals of Major Samuel Shaw

# 36. The American Army Suffers at Valley Forge

*Washington's army, defeated by Howe at the battle of Brandywine on September 11, 1777, was compelled to retire beyond Philadelphia while the British entered that city. The Continental Congress fled first to Lancaster and then to*

*York in Pennsylvania. Meanwhile the British fleet held Delaware Bay and captured Forts Mercer and Mifflin. All the maritime areas of Rhode Island, New York, Delaware, and Pennsylvania were thus in the hands of the royal forces. For the darkest winter of the war, Washington settled down with his fragmentary army at Valley Forge. But somehow the army got through that winter and emerged stronger and better disciplined than it had ever been.*

SAND and forest, forest and sand, formed the whole way from Williamsburg to the camp at Valley Forge. I do not remember how many days I took to accomplish this difficult journey. Being badly fed, as a natural consequence I walked badly, and passed at least six nights under the trees through not meeting with any habitation. Not knowing the language, I often strayed from the right road, which was so much time and labor lost. At last, early in November [1777], I arrived at Valley Forge.

The American army was then encamped three or four leagues from Philadelphia, which city was then occupied by the British, who were rapidly fulfilling the prophecy of Dr. Franklin.

That celebrated man — an ambassador who amused himself with science, which he adroitly made to assist him in his diplomatic work — said, when some friends came to Passy to condole with him on the fall of Philadelphia: "You are mistaken; it is not the British army that has taken Philadelphia, but Philadelphia that has taken the British army." The cunning old diplomatist was right. The capital of Pennsylvania had already done for the British what Capua did in a few months for the soldiers of Hannibal. The Americans — the "insurgents" as they were called — camped at Valley Forge; the British officers, who were in the city, gave themselves up to pleasure; there were continual balls and other amusements; the troops were idle and enervated by inaction, and the generals undertook nothing all the winter.

Soon I came in sight of the camp. My imagination had pictured an army with uniforms, the glitter of arms, standards, etc., in short, military pomp of all sorts. Instead of the imposing spectacle I expected, I saw, grouped together or standing alone, a few militiamen, poorly clad, and for the most part without shoes — many of them badly armed, but all well supplied with provisions, and I noticed that tea and sugar formed part of their rations. I did not then know that this was not unusual, and I laughed, for it made me think of the recruiting sergeants on the Quai de la Ferraille at Paris, who say to the yokels, "You will want for nothing when you are in the regiment, but if bread should run short you must not mind eating cakes." Here the soldiers had tea and sugar. In passing through the camp I also noticed soldiers wearing cotton nightcaps under their hats, and some having for cloaks or greatcoats coarse woolen blankets, exactly like those provided for the patients in our French hospitals. I learned afterwards that these were the officers and generals.

Such, in strict truth, was, at the time I came amongst them, the appearance of this armed mob, the leader of whom was the man who has rendered the name of Washington famous; such were the colonists — unskilled warriors who learned in a few years how to conquer the finest troops that England could send against them. Such also, at the beginning of the War of Independence, was the state of want in the insurgent army, and such was the scarcity of money, and the poverty of that government, now so rich, powerful, and prosperous, that its notes, called Continental paper money, were nearly valueless.

THE CHEVALIER DE PONTGIBAUD, A French Volunteer of the War of Independence

# 37. George Rogers Clark Conquers the Northwest

*The British forts on the Wabash and Mississippi were small, but they enabled British agents to incite the Indians north of the Ohio River to attack American settlers in the West. To put an end to this George Rogers Clark, a Virginian settled in Kentucky, led a force westward in 1778 and took Kaskaskia and Cahokia. Little fighting was required, for the small British gar-*

*risons were dependent on the good will of the French settlers about.*
*When late in 1778 the British commander at Detroit, Henry Hamil-*
*ton, recovered Vincennes on the Wabash, Clark resolved upon instant*
*counter measures. Early in February, 1779, he set out from Kaskaskia*
*on the Mississippi to retake Vincennes and Fort Sackville, held by*
*only about eighty men.*

EVERYTHING being ready, on the 5th of February [1779]
after receiving a lecture and absolution from a priest, we crossed the
Kaskaskia River with one hundred and seventy men and at a
distance of about three miles encamped until February 8. When we
again resumed the advance the weather was wet and a part of
the country was covered with several inches of water. Progress
under these conditions was difficult and fatiguing, although, fortunately, it was not very cold considering the time of year. My object now was to keep the men in good spirits. I permitted them to
shoot game on all occasions and to feast on it like Indians at a war
dance, each company taking turns in inviting the other to its
feast. A feast was held every night, the company that was to give
it being always supplied with horses for laying in a sufficient
store of meat in the course of the day. I myself and my principal
officers conducted ourselves like woodsmen, shouting now and
then and running through the mud and water the same as the men
themselves.

Thus, insensible of their hardships and without complaining, our
men were conducted through difficulties far surpassing anything we
had ever experienced before this, to the banks of the Little Wabash,
which we reached on February 13. There are here two streams
three miles apart, and the distance from the bank of one to the
opposite bank of the other is five miles. This whole distance we
found covered with some three feet of water, being never less than
two and frequently four feet in depth. I went into camp on an
elevation at the bank of the river and gave the troops permission
to amuse themselves. For some time I viewed with consternation
this expanse of water; then, accusing myself of irresolution, without holding any consultation over the situation or permitting any

one else to do so in my presence, I immediately set to work. I ordered a pirogue to be constructed at once and acted as though crossing the water would be only a bit of diversion. Since but few of the men could find employment at a time, pains were taken to devise amusement for the rest in order to keep up their spirits. However, the men were well prepared for the undertaking before us as they had frequently waded farther than we must now, although seldom in water more than half-leg-deep. . . .

On the evening of the 14th our boat was completed and I sent a crew of men to explore the drowned lands and find if possible some spot of dry land on the bank of the second little river. They found a place about half an acre in extent and marked the trees from it back to the camp. They returned with a very favorable report, having received private instructions from me in advance as to what they should say.

Fortunately for us the 15th chanced to be a warm, moist day, considering the season. The channel of the river where we were encamped was about thirty yards wide and the opposite bank was under three feet of water. Here we built a scaffold and the baggage was put upon it and ferried across, while our horses swam the channel and at the scaffold were again loaded with the baggage. By this time the soldiers had also been brought across and we took up our march, our boat being loaded with men who were sick.

We proceeded down below the mouth of the Embarrass, vainly attempting to reach the banks of the Wabash. Finding a dry spot, we encamped late at night and in the morning were gratified at hearing for the first time the morning gun of the British garrison. We resumed our march and about two o'clock in the afternoon of the 18th gained the banks of the Wabash, three leagues below the town, and went into camp.

On the 20th the water guard decoyed a boat ashore, having five Frenchmen and some provisions on board. These men were on their way down-river to join a party of hunters. They informed us that we had been discovered and that the inhabitants were well disposed toward us.

The men we had captured said it was impossible for us to make the town that night, or at all with our boats. Recalling what we